Australian Biographical Monographs

11

Australian Biographical Monographs
Series Editor: Scott Prasser

Previous Volumes

1. *Joseph Lyons and the Management of Adversity* — Kevin Andrews

2. *Harold Holt and the Liberal Imagination* — Tom Frame

3. *Johannes Bjelke-Petersen* — Bruce Kingston

4. *Lindsay Thompson Character, Competence and Conviction* — William Westerman

5. *Neville Wran* — David Clune

6. *Robert Menzies Man or Myth* — Scott Prasser

7. *Stanley Melbourne Bruce Institution Builder* — David Lee

8. *John Grey Gorton Australian to the Bootheels: The paradoxical life of Gorton* — Paul Williams

9. *Sir Robert Askin* — Paul Loughnan

10. *George Reid* — Luke Walker

Australian Biographical Monographs

11

Neville Bonner

Sean Jacobs

Connor Court Publishing

Published in 2021 by Connor Court Publishing Pty Ltd

Copyright © Sean Jacobs 2021

All rights reserved. No part of this book may be reproduced or transmitted in any form or by any means, electronic or mechanical, including photo copying, recording or by any information storage and retrieval system, without prior permission in writing from the publisher.

Connor Court Publishing Pty Ltd
PO Box 7257
Redland Bay QLD 4165
sales@connorcourt.com
www.connorcourt.com
Phone 0497-900-685

Printed in Australia

ISBN:9781922449719

Front cover design: Maria Giordano

Front cover picture: Wikipedia Commons.

"Forget Neville Bonner as the person, the major thing was that for the first time in history, an Indigenous person had made it into the federal parliament where all laws pertaining to this nation are made... I spoke as an Indigenous person. I spoke as an ordinary, average Australian, albeit Aborigine."

Neville Bonner, 1995.

Acknowledgement

I would like to sincerely thank Nathaniel Brown, Jason Deutsch, Anthony Dillon, David Flint, Jacqueline and Victoria Jacobs, and Nigel Parbury, for reading early drafts and offering comments. These people, in their precious spare time, have spotted my errors and offered gentle and constructive advice. Anthony Cappello and Scott Prasser have also been instrumental in ensuring this important story receives a platform. I also thank my wife Eloise for her constant patience and encouragement. The views expressed and any errors are entirely my own.

Series overview

The Connor Court *Australian Biographical Series* focusses on important Australian political leaders and other major figures. It seeks to provide an overview for those who are unfamiliar with the subject, and to highlight the person's particular importance, controversies around them and their contribution to Australia's progress.

The monographs are scholarly rather than academic in focus, placing emphasis on a clear narrative, but with careful attention to sources to ensure views expressed are appropriately supported.

The Series was initiated because of the decline in the study of Australian history at our schools and universities and the consequential lack of knowledge or, even worse, distorting of views, of some of Australia's leading historical figures who deserve to be remembered, understood for their achievements, and, as each volume also highlights, their flaws.

Neville Bonner was partly selected because he was the first Indigenous federal parliamentarian, filling a casual vacancy to the Senate for the Liberal Party in 1971 and subsequently elected in his own right until 1983.

But he was more than that. Born under a tree in northern New South Wales to later serve at the highest levels of Australian politics, Bonner shows us that working 'within the system', from the inside, carried more potency than trying to tear it down and start again – a very real impulse for the leading voices of his time. His difficult journey represents a positive perspective on the importance of everyday people offering a 'hand up', the best parts of Australia's history, and the need to balance culture and heritage to prosper in a modern world.

This new meticulously researched monograph by Papua New Guinean-born Sean Jacobs shows us that optimism and effort, paired with belief and aspiration, can set you up on the right course in life. We come to understand Bonner the man and the circumstances that shaped him along the way. Bonner's principles and beliefs, now forgotten by some, are more relevant than ever.

Why Bonner?

Most of us can recall our first day at school. Or, if not, the Sunday night before starting a new job. The slight anxiety of stepping into something new for the first time. The tingling of the nerves. The inability, as many of us might experience, to catch a proper night's sleep. Or to simply worry what others might think.

It's highly likely that similar feelings governed a tiny Neville Bonner, accompanied by his young brother and sister, fronting up to a first day at South Lismore School in the early 1930s. A wonderful image – three bright-eyed blackfella kids, living under lantana and flimsy corrugated iron on the Richmond River, eagerly on their way to a whitefella school.

The enrolment, brokered by the local police sergeant and school principal, offered a rare but important occasion. Bonner's mother – Julia – had not been able to afford school uniforms. But "handy using cotton and needles" she'd managed to trim down sets of old worn pants and fashioned shirts, literally from inside-out sacks, to ensure the Bonners presented as smart as possible on their important first day.[1]

"We arrived at school at about eight o'clock in the morning, half past eight," Bonner recalled from relative comfort years later, "and by the time school started, we were the only three children left at school."[2] Word had gone viral – at least by 1930s standards – that "we black kids were there" and parents had shepherded their children away in time for the opening bell.[3]

"Look," said the Headmaster finally, "I'm sorry children, you'll have to go home."[4] Unthinkable now but, back then, par for the course.

Such heartbreak, at the starting line of a long and challenging life, says so much about Australia's first Indigenous parliamentarian – the towering dignity to keep rocking up, to be a full participant in an at times difficult society, to twice attempt World War Two enlistment and, after countless more indignities, represent the State of Queensland as a conservative politician for 12 years in the national parliament.

I decided to put together this short biography of Neville Bonner because his story says so much, not just about a good man, but about a good country. In his later years Bonner recalled how Australia had, despite its faults, improved a great deal in his lifetime. Decent democracies seem to evolve that way – always striving, even in dark days, toward higher principles. Bonner knew that, beneath the layers of liberal contradictions and hypocrisy, there lay the Aussie 'fair go' – a principled pluralism, a sturdy constitution, 'wealth for toil', the safety net of strong communities and, most importantly in his life, the presence of good people.

Indeed, good people were the antidote to Bonner's many collisions with racial misery. "They tried to get me to hate white people," said the black American jazz musician Thelonious Monk, "but someone would always come along and spoil it." Bonner's experience followed a similar line. His deep belief in the goodness of Australians, and what Australia stood for, would serve Bonner more than well, not just in dealing with the arrows of discrimination and segregation, but walking between black and white, radicals and conformists, federalists and centralists and, eventually, prime ministers and premiers. Despite an early life of genuine hard knocks, and a career of being stretched between competing political dynamics, he possessed that great Australian trait to remain optimistic and not carry an ounce of real cynicism.

Why else write about Bonner? First, rather selfishly, he has been a hero of mine. While not an Indigenous Australian, I am also mixed-race – having an European father and Papua New Guinean mother. I first discovered his biography when stumbling through a Canberra library as a young policy adviser at the Department of the Prime Minister and Cabinet. A true trailblazer, he has been a great reminder that you don't have to look like the people in your industry, sector, workplace or community to fit in, contribute or add value.

Second, Bonner is a good example in showing how identity politics, with its poisonous resentments and aggressive intolerance, can only take one so far. Bonner, after all, was an individual who chose 'compromise over confrontation'. He was proud of his Aboriginality but realised cultural identity required balance in a modern world – not leaving cultural identity at the door but acknowledging that being 'part and parcel' of the Australian community was his overall goal. And that working 'within the system', as we say, from the inside, carried more potency than trying to tear it down and start again – a very real impulse for the radicals of his day. He is a great example of persistence and 'by the bootstraps' upward mobility in the difficult era he lived. So why not dust this off and retell this story today?

Third, despite how far Australia has come in terms of wiping out discrimination and segregation, Bonner's story stays relevant, but not always in the way we might like it to be. We can't deny that huge strides forward have been made in removing discriminatory practice and legislation in the affairs of government, and in our social lives, elevating individual dignity over complexion. Rather than fading away as a subject, however, I've learnt that writing about race in Australia is never quite out of vogue and near-seasonal in nature – cohesive and serene one minute, fragmenting and feverish the next. Although I don't quite wish it, there's always a relevant time to write about race.

So great leaps forward have been made. But some of these are off a higher bar than we might imagine. Bonner's story dispels some myths on 'backward' Queensland as the 'deep north'. Upon close consideration, it is no accident that Bonner was a Queenslander and emerged from the conservative side of politics. After all, practical conservative politics, at least in Queensland, places the highest premium on the individual. And it was the state of Queensland, Bonner said, where all complexions could prosper with hard work and an enterprising spirit. Studied more closely, it isn't too contradictory that such a state produced the first Indigenous parliamentarian and not the southern and supposedly more progressive and cosmopolitan states.

Fourth, his story underlines the decency of our institutions, raising the appeal of politics at a time when we repel it so much. Australians have, for good reason, always de-romanticised politics. But in thinking of Bonner we can remind ourselves to briefly lift our gaze and see it as a place for good.

Finally, I wanted to place Bonner's life and story in one accessible place. There is some very good information on Bonner – a neat 1979 biography by journalist Angela Burger, a well-written Senate biography by academic Tim Rowse, a number of oral history interviews, Hansard and a handful of delicate and reflective condolence motions following Bonner's death on 5 February 1999. A few years ago, I wrote on his inspirational legacy for the Centre for Independent Studies' (CIS's) now defunct *Policy* magazine.

But I feel there is a curious under-acknowledgement of Bonner's place in our history. He is not a figure that historians, or modern current affairs commentators, have fallen over themselves to examine in depth or to elevate in profile. Some offer an easy but misguided narrative to Bonner – he was a black man who ultimately became trapped by white conservative politics. Others tend to side-step his philosophy, which did not align with the Indigenous separatism that accompanied the Indigenous rights movement of the 1960s and 70s – and is rampant now.

In the CIS piece I suggested that Bonner's conservatism – his proud allegiance to the Liberal Party and distrust of radicalism – has suspiciously camouflaged his legacy. More radical figures tend to capture our historical memories. With time I have grown weary of this explanation but, politics aside, the outcome of Bonner's relatively slim legacy ends up in the same place. There are no grand anthologies or serious attempts to show how a complex black character – in the pivotal era of civil rights – carries huge relevance for our modern trials around social cohesion and the legitimacy of our public institutions. This is especially the case when we are slowly drowning in rabid identity politics and needing, more than ever, to broadcast individual achievers overcoming the odds and prospering.

As a brief illustration, a few years ago I wrote a short piece for a US publication – *Hip Hop Republican* – noting the parallels between Bonner and the former American slave and educator Booker T Washington. Both men, although from vastly different contexts and times, display overwhelming similarities – espousing individualism, reviling self-pity, constantly emphasising good character and working 'within the system' – regardless of the injustices of the day. The self-agency message of 'Booker T' – as Washington is widely known – enjoys strong prevalence among Americans in a way that Bonner does not in this country. This, some might say, is due to the ruthless pragmatism of Australian politics and not lionising our politicians. And if this short biographical profile can help turn this around, albeit slightly, I hope it is a worthwhile outcome.

The former British Prime Minister Tony Blair said he wrote his autobiography thematically "rather than following a precise chronology."[5] This, he says, was to "avoid trailing off in desperation" and to "keep the same pace and energy throughout."[6] I will attempt to follow Blair's approach here. I am also not a professional historian, as the saying goes, but a student of history. This means any mistakes are my own.

In 1993, upon receiving his honorary doctorate from Griffith University, Bonner said that a piano, like a society, sounds best when the black and white keys are played together. It is simple advice that reflects the tone of Bonner's life and, ultimately, the timeless ideas he stood for. Doing so was a bumpy ride. But a ride that has shown us so much.

What to do with grievance?

Today we are becoming accustomed to outbreaks of acute racial sensitivity – trigger warnings, microaggressions, the need for safe spaces. In the United States, for example, stepping out in the wrong

Halloween costume can get you into serious trouble. Western classics can be viewed as unsuitable for some minority university students, or at least front-ended with heavy caveats, to ensure minimal harm or offence. Some speakers, particularly those with a conservative tilt, are often shut down from speaking or answering questions at leading campuses.

These are elements of what American scholars Jonathan Haidt and Greg Lukianoff call "vindictive protectiveness" – protecting someone from harm by "attacking the aggressor".[7] It is a harmful trend that Australia is yet to *fully* import.

But the parallels are slowly growing. Monash University has adopted a trigger warning policy and other institutions are following suit. The Australian National University's rejection of the Ramsay Centre for Western Civilisation's undergraduate degree symbolised the modern scepticism of Western studies. And conservative speakers, or at least those challenging progressive ideas, have found speaking on some Australian campuses extremely difficult. These initiatives, slow but seemingly inevitable in their import, have all linked back to the idea of removing any threat of emotional distress, anxiety or trauma – or even challenge – from the next generation of minds.

Contrast this with Neville Bonner – a man who grew up without the safety net or 'cover' that such policies supposedly provide. Born in 1922 on Ukerebagh Island, northern New South Wales, Bonner spent his early life living under metal sheeting and lantana bushes on the bank of Lismore's Wilsons River. His mother – Julia – gave birth to him, literally, under the foot of a tree. "That I and she both survived is a miracle," said Bonner in 1992, "when I heard the stories of what was happening at Ukerebagh Island in those days."[8]

Indeed, it is hard to believe that, not just within our lifetimes, but in a place as prosperous as Australia, an individual could be born into such conditions. Bonner's mother Julia, originally from South Queensland's Deebing Creek, was not a local to the area and he never met his English father – Henry Bonner – who left just after Neville was born. Julia then linked up with Frank Randell – a local blacktracker with the police. His connections weren't without benefit, appearing to facilitate their move from Ukerebagh Island to Lismore and leading to Bonner's very short-lived stint at South Lismore Public School.

In Lismore, Bonner and his brother Henry walked two miles each day with their mother to help wash sheets at a local motel. This would not have been an easy commute for Julia, limping for most of her life after falling out of a tree as a child. The Bonner boys also took trips to Lismore town, where they would "call at houses to ask the housewives if they had any jobs for two strong fellows."[9]

Sadly in 1933, while Bonner was just eleven, Julia passed away and the children fell under the guardianship of their grandparents. If young Bonner's short-lived attempt at school wasn't heartbreaking enough, the first time he ate porridge would have landed an equally crushing blow. Laced with weevils, but a rare privilege not easily dismissed, Grandmother Ida had thoughtfully brought it home to share with the young boys. "White people have it for breakfast," said Ida, "but they have it with *milk*," she emphasised. So an enterprising young Bonner, marching up to the nearest dairy farm, beamed with pride as he asked a local farmer for a jug of his finest produce. "I felt so proud we were having porridge for breakfast," he said.

His youthful enthusiasm, however, quickly evaporated. "Be off with you, you little black bugger," yelled the farmer. "My milk is for the pigs."[10]

Such moments, as psychologists remind us, can crush us for life. But there are two life-long reflections when we learn of Bonner's early setbacks. The first is a near meditative, and even empathetic, reflection on his formative years. "It was a hard life, but good training," he told his biographer Angela Burger in the late 1970s. "We learned we had to work for anything we wanted. No one cared very much about Aborigines then, but we managed. Some of us have done well; some have not. When I think back on those years, I have to say they stood me in good stead."[11] Even the local dairy farmer received Bonner's empathy. "I suppose it was fair enough," said Bonner. "He could fatten his pigs for sale and he couldn't make a profit out of me. He was looking after himself and devil take the hindmost."[12]

The second and more direct political observation is that Bonner did not become overly consumed by radical activism, which was the prevailing posture of the Indigenous rights movement of the 1960s and 70s – the years of his political awakening and ascendance. "The insults he suffered as a black child in a white world," observed a 1971 news article – the year Bonner became a Senator – "could easily have made him a bitter supporter of militant 'black power'."[13]

Although from different contexts, Australia's Black Power movement borrowed directly from American rhetoric and its techniques. Indigenous activist Charles Perkins, echoing Montgomery, Alabama, organised bus boycotts and freedom marches. Roberta Sykes, the first black Australian to graduate from an American university, championed Indigenous activism and helped lead the landmark 1972 Aboriginal Tent Embassy protests in Canberra – protestors who would clash with Bonner in his first year as a Senator. Indeed, social protest and agitation would shape Bonner's era of politics in Australia, and politics across the Western world.

Yet Bonner seemed to understand the tension, and at times the yawning chasm, between protest and compromise. He took the moral agenda of the civil rights era – an end to segregation and discrimination – but clearly aimed to achieve this through compromise rather than confrontation. In doing so, he went on to live a life mercifully free of the prevailing attitude of entitlement or never-ending rights we see today.

Racial culpability as a means of advancement didn't quite square with him. He would say, often under attack from activists, that he was trying to do the same things – achieve change – but by different means and through the Australian Parliament and our other established institutions. "We do not want an Aboriginal parliament," he would tell the Senate. "We want to be part and parcel of the Australian community. We want to see more Aborigines in this chamber."[14]

Rather than an indictment of Australian history, which is where a great deal of Indigenous history can end up today, there is something decent about Bonner's lessons that we can apply to our contemporary challenges – finding empathy, distrusting radicalism, seeing the best in our institutions and elevating dignity under fire. These civic ideas can not only ward off 'vindictive protectiveness' but help to improve ourselves, remind us of greater ideals and enhance our democracy.

60,000 years in a lifetime

I was born in Port Moresby, Papua New Guinea (PNG), in the mid-1980s. My mother is from the remote island of New Hanover – a three-hour boat ride from the nearest airstrip – in PNG's north eastern New Ireland Province.

When I was born, PNG's total population was around 3.9 million. Today it has more than doubled and, in recent years, the country has been one of the fastest growing economies in the world. Despite such growth it's still sometimes common, at least in remote areas, for some Papua New Guinean children to not have seen a white person before – an experience I've observed even among members of my own family. Over time I've paid close attention to PNG navigating high population growth and economic globalisation – the challenges it brings, the wealth it creates, the inequities it exposes and, most importantly, the hard questions it asks about culture in responding to the modern world.

One of PNG's founding fathers – the late Albert Maori Kiki – titled his 1965 autobiography *10,000 Years in a Lifetime*. Kiki, from the Orokolo village in PNG's Gulf District, captured the challenges of traditional custom – initiation rituals, messages from the dead, not stealing another man's pig – running into the stuffy attitudes of PNG's Australian-ruled colonial era. It was the perfect title for PNG's lurch to modernity and, for a relatively young nation, the game of 'catch-up' required among everyday Papua New Guineans and their distinctively British institutions.

I've often thought how Kiki's stories and ideas would transfer to the history of Indigenous Australians. Indeed, all the elements are there. The title of this chapter would certainly be fitting. But the theme of culture colliding with modernity, and with European contact, follows similar riffs. The nature of this early contact says so much about continental Indigenous Australians prior to the First Fleet's landing in 1788.

And it says so much about assimilation and other discomforting challenges presenting in Bonner's early life and throughout his political career.

Here a very brief look at Indigenous and external contact is required. Various explorers prodded parts of the continent, from Dutchman Willem Janszoon to Spaniard Luis Vaz de Torres. Even the Chinese are believed to have reached the east coast sometime between 206 BC and AD 220, as well the Portuguese many centuries later. In all instances the continent inspired very little. In 1644, in terms of human contact, the Dutch seafarer Abel Tasman observed uncharitably from the coast "naked beach-roving wretches, destitute even of rice... miserably poor, and in many places of a very bad disposition."[15] American Indians had lived for 14,000 years prior to contact. PNG, as Kiki suggests, 10,000. But 60,000?[16] Indigenous Australians were in a league of their own.

By 1788, as Arthur Phillip led the First Fleet into Sydney Cove, Britain was in the throes of the Industrial Revolution. Machines had already taken the place of hand production – huge leaps forward in terms of innovation. But the continent he was pulling into was, as one Australian historian notes, a place where "not a wheel had turned, no permanent structures existed and agriculture was unknown."[17] The reason for this, as Bonner explained in his maiden speech, was because "my people had simple needs. We saw no need for agriculture or industry because nature provided our needs for over 20,000 years."[18] Bonner, incidentally, underestimated his people's habitation in Australia, as did everyone before the most recent archaeological discoveries.

There are many accounts of 'first contacts' between black and white. After reading many accounts of these it is hard to go past the Australian historian Geoffrey Bolton's highly blunt observation:

> *When after 1788 the two cultures came into close contact there was no real prospect that they could achieve mutual understanding, still less that the technically superior Europeans would dream that they had anything to learn from the Aborigines about the care and control of the Australian environment... the Aborigines in all their centuries of occupation contented themselves with the lives of nomadic hunters, merely scratching the surface of the continent.*[19]

That Indigenous Australians not only survived, but in fact lived well with the land for tens of thousands of years is universally applauded. But 'nomadic hunting', far from a simple anthropological observation, presented complications for Indigenous Australians at the time of settlement and especially as the colonies grew.

The most obvious challenge has been around land. Britain at the time of Australian settlement placed a significant premium on private property. Stealing a pig or chicken in Britain, for example, could meet the punishment of harsh exile to Australia. But tangible ground – Enlightenment thinker John Locke's mixing of 'labour with the soil' – remained a key objective for the thousands of Brits and others streaming out of a crowded Britain into the expanding colonies. Except no equal instinct – a Lockean commitment to tilling solid ground – had emerged among Indigenous Australians. "If we stayed in the one place and killed everything," noted Bonner, "that would be the end of it. We rotated around allowing nature to provide and crops to rejuvenate."[20]

It wouldn't have been easy for colonial authorities, tested not only by increasing numbers of insatiable immigrants but maintaining control over an ever-expanding frontier, and an Indigenous population – with 60,000 years of tradition – moving across fence-lines and boundaries. Successive authorities set aside parcels of land as reserves, arrived at mechanisms of compensation and designed laws to protect and, ostensibly, control.

In Queensland, this would mean creating instruments like the *Aboriginals Protection and Restriction of the Sale of Opium Act 1897*. Strangely named, its full title, or at least the former part of it, reflected thinking at the time – *A Bill to make Provision for the better Protection and Care of the Aboriginal and Half-caste Inhabitants of the Colony, and to make more effectual Provision for Restricting the Sale and Distribution of Opium*. Far from being relegated to history, the 1897 Act had changed to appear, in Bonner's time, as *The Queensland Aborigines' and Torres Strait Islanders' Affairs Act 1965* – also known as the Queensland Act.

This governed Indigenous reserves and regulated the overall control of Indigenous Queenslanders.

And while its removal was encouraged, and Bonner deeply felt that Indigenous Australians should be 'part and parcel of the Australian community', he was also aware of the damaging consequences of abruptly removing legislation that had been in place for well over half a century. "I don't think protection can be lifted at once," he said. "It may be three or four generations before our people can have complete independence with no settlements, no special legislation and no allocation of funds."[21]

This is an entirely admirable goal – a commitment to a genuine equality – and one that is critical to understanding Bonner. As he rose in politics, and as a Senator, his legislative agenda appeared at times incoherent – crossing the floor thirty-four times – and appearing in support of Queensland one minute, and Canberra the next. While not always easy to see, integration and the 'equality agenda' – no settlements, no special legislation and no special funding – remained a central objective of Bonner's. He was a strong supporter of state rights but, importantly, local decisions being made as close to the people affected as possible. And he appeared to genuinely examine issues on their merits, unafraid in offering his view, and possessing an independent mind.

But even well before he considered becoming a federal Senator, he had a very long way to go.

Education

Despite only a year of formal education at Queensland's Beaudesert Rural State School, Bonner was an eloquent man. He'd say, over the years, that he fooled many by being well-spoken.

He owed this eloquence to his Grandma – Ida – who looked after him when Julia passed away. "Everything I have achieved or am ever likely to achieve, Granny Ida was the start of it all," said Bonner. "She wanted so much for me... she was a disciplinarian, but she never smacked us."[22] There's something common to Granny Ida's approach – a mix of discipline with higher expectations – that propels the young underprivileged on to bigger and better things. This is particularly observable with many black conservatives.

The American neurosurgeon and republican presidential contender Ben Carson, for example, anchors his success to his mother's discipline, who 'marked up' many of his junior school essays despite not being able to read. The mere illusion of her fake pen strokes, notes Carson, was enough to sharpen his performance – an early move that would see him become a world leader in the surgical separation of conjoined twins and a serious United States presidential contender.

A similar story is seen with the noted black American and author of *The Content of Our Character*, Shelby Steele. Growing up in segregated Chicago, Illinois, Steele recorded his frustrations as a young man confronted by a white female teacher for his bad grammar and use of language. Annoyed one day at her constant corrections, Steele lazily accused her of racism. It wasn't met well. "She said she didn't give a 'good goddamn' about my race," recounted Steele, "but that if I wanted to do more than 'sweat my life away in a steel mill,' I better learn to speak correctly."[23] Higher expectations pushed him on to bigger things.

Bonner's command of English was also a ticket to something better. And while his formal schooling may have been cut short, it didn't result in a predictable advocacy for more funding and greater government control of education – things we tend to automatically expect from the significantly underprivileged.

Here some context is helpful. In 1971 – the year Bonner became a Senator – Australian education was in its watershed phase. Labor's Gough Whitlam, replacing Liberal William McMahon as prime minister in 1972, was responsible for an unprecedented expansion in educational expenditure. To be fair, this had been started by the Liberal giant Robert Menzies' nod toward funding non-government schools in the previous decade – a trend continued and expanded by his successors.

Although well-intentioned, it represented a departure from 90 years of precedent. And it offered a political gift to Whitlam – a politician more than enthusiastic about the capacity of government to shape outcomes and offer opportunities. Increased spending on education "must be done," he said in his famous 1972 'It's Time' speech, "not just because the basic resource of this nation is the skills of its people, but because education is the key to equality of opportunity."[24] Whitlam clearly inspired Australians at the time with fresh themes of change.

But half a century later, it's not too hard to see where his commitment to government largesse, and education, has over-tilted – too many university spaces, for example, and not enough jobs requiring a university education. Only 75 percent of recent university graduates, according to one analysis, have actually found full-time work – a trend that doesn't appear to be improving.[25] When it comes to teaching as a profession itself, the education bubble hasn't just ballooned outward but inward. As Australian writer David Gillespie notes, in New South Wales alone there are:

> ... about 33,000 people on the waiting list for a job as a teacher in a government school. But those schools have a total teaching workforce of just 49,000 and create just 2000 jobs a year as a result of retirements and resignations. Meanwhile, approximately 6000 new teaching graduates will be added to the list each year.[26]

Despite being only a newcomer to the Senate, Bonner was alive to these trends, forecasting the shortfalls of Whitlam's education approach and the problems it would bring. Standing in the Chamber in 1974, Bonner criticised the dependency and lack of choice Whitlam's education policies were creating:

> *The Government adopts the attitude: 'Big Brother will look after you. You must send your children to a government school'. The fact that people in the community prefer to send their children either to a religious school or to some private school, for reasons of their own, does not matter to this Government. It says: 'If you want any assistance, you must send them to government schools.'*[27]

In the same speech, he reminded the Chamber that not all private school parents were bathing in wealth. Many, he noted, had moved mountains in sending their children to private schools:

> *The Government speaks about wealthy schools. Why are the schools wealthy? They are wealthy because people have worked and have made sacrifices to that their children will get the best education money can provide. Nevertheless, these people must contribute to the nation's economy through taxes. That is another example of the hypocrisy of this Government in its attitude towards education. Yet it tries to blow its own trumpet and say what a wonderful job it is doing.*[28]

Bonner also recalled, in later years, that 'spending big' on education, because of its administrative intensity, didn't necessarily trickle down to outcomes at the student level. "They say 'Billions of dollars spent on education'," he lamented. "But how much of it is spent on education. The teachers, the inspectors and all the staff. Look at all the money that goes into that. But you've still got to have them to have educated children."[29]

'Teacher to student ratios' also didn't escape Bonner's critique. It seems having less students per teacher is a common sense idea, at least on face value. But not always, as Bonner explained:

> When I think of the little bit of schooling I had in New South Wales, there was one teacher and she taught first, second, third, fourth grades or classes. One teacher. She had about 40 kids. She taught the lot. Teachers now have one subject and they can't have more than 25 children. Now, does that mean that the people of the day are less intelligent than Mrs Hiscock was? Less capable that Mrs Hiscock was? After all, I had a short time with her and I became a Senator. So God bless her![30]

Despite Bonner's foresight, there are two education issues that he didn't, or couldn't, anticipate at the time – the relaxation of standards at Australian universities and the scepticism regarding Western studies.

Steady analysis, even prior to Covid-19, has shown the single-commodity reliance of Australian universities on Asian students. This has thrown further light on the alarming rate at which foreign students are being 'pushed through' qualifications with a very limited command of English. Bonner also noted the difficulties Indigenous students faced with both standards and language. These students, he said, faced enormous hurdles "when they go into schools which are conducted under the white man's educational system," adding that the challenges "must be doubled or trebled for the Aboriginal children who live in a tribal or semi-tribal state and who speak or who have learned to speak nothing other than their own tongue."[31]

For Bonner, to not only speak English but to speak it *well* represented a mark of educational accomplishment – one he clearly didn't have on paper – but also a capacity to participate, learn and exchange in a free and open society. The modern education technique of 'immersion' – where Indigenous language comes first and English second – wouldn't have won Bonner's approval.

A proud Jagera elder, he was a man more than proud of his Aboriginality but understood a good education was critical to thrive in the modern world. He was saddened by the decline of cultural practice, noting later in life that the Indigenous artists Yothu Yindi had become more popular in the United Kingdom than in Bonner's hometown of Ipswich.

I sense the other trend – a scepticism of Western studies – would have equally puzzled Bonner. As Bonner's parliamentary colleague Senator Fred Chaney observed – "A full Western education – education to understand and to be able to function in the post-Enlightenment world – is a necessity for Aboriginal survival."[32] Bonner would not have disagreed, encouraging not just Indigenous Australians, but all young Australians, to learn to be able to thrive and do well in our more prosperous times.

It was the American president Calvin Coolidge who famously said "Nothing in this world can take the place of persistence," adding that "Education will not; the world is full of educated derelicts."[33] Bonner clearly had persistence. Not so much to be a Senator, especially in his early years, but to merely earn a decent living and survive.

And here we turn to Bonner's classroom – the school of hard knocks, he said, and where experience was his teacher.

The philosophy of Tommy Bell

Bonner, from northern New South Wales to central Queensland, seemed to work every job known to man. Some accounts say he was a scrub-feller and meat worker.[34] Others that he was a 'stockman' or found odd jobs on plantations.[35]

The truth is all of the above. From fifteen, he 'carried a swag' – as the saying goes – mainly throughout Queensland cutting chaff, picking gooseberries, clearing lantana, handling cattle, riding horses, fencing, and working as a station hand and stockman. He even helped string a telephone line from Redcliffe to Cocklebinda in Queensland's north.

But his occupation as a dairy hand was *the* skill he'd return to over the years. After a brief stint at school in Beaudesert, he found a job working on a dairy farm just outside of town. At night he earned extra money by cutting chaff. This gave him two to three shillings on top of his weekly wage of five shillings.

Bonner enjoyed being around people – he didn't seem to relish solitude, especially in his younger years. Unable to stand the loneliness on the dairy farm, he moved to Wiangaree, northern New South Wales, reuniting with his brother Henry. For two years he again plied his skills by working on a dairy farm.

It is well known that work is a great moral educator. And Bonner was taking on a great moral education.

It was at this time, in around 1937, that his Uncle Jack arrived from Woorabinda – an Indigenous settlement 178 kilometres south west of Rockhampton – and convinced Bonner to move back with him. Bonner agreed. Slowly paying their way by picking gooseberries and clearing lantana, they threaded their way up through northern New South Wales and southern Queensland back toward the small Aboriginal township. Clearing lantana had paid well. With a few pounds for a few months of work, they purchased bikes and rode 600 kilometres north – enough for two stages of the Tour de France – before finally arriving at Woorabinda.

It was here, Bonner said, where he experienced his first taste of settlement life – a white superintendent, white administrative staff and native police. Until then, he had lived outside the ordered regimentation of the black-white divide. It was also in Woorabinda where he first began to properly witness and appreciate tribal custom of the local Wadja Wadja and Yungulu people. Again, he put his skills to work and returned to a dairy farm, now earning eight shillings a fortnight.

After a short time, Bonner was sent to Cocklebinda, west of Biloela, to handle cattle and ride horses. Edward Palmer, in his 1903 book *Early Days in North Queensland*, wrote that Indigenous youth were clearly great trackers but also made "the best all-round stockman; many follow horse-breaking at times, or take a turn at droving."[36] It's hard to find a young and vigorous Bonner defying this image.

It was at around this time that he helped Alf and Jim O'Rourke clear scrub and milk cattle. In 1974, as a Senator, Bonner returned to Biloela and was formally welcomed by Alf O'Rourke – by then a Councillor and Chairman of the Banana Shire Council. "Good morning Senator," beamed Cr O'Rourke, no doubt with cap in hand. "I welcome you to my Shire. It is a great pleasure to meet you."[37] Bonner, stepping back, cautiously raised his eyebrows before breaking into a smile, "Oh don't be so bloody silly Alf, you old nigger driver," he said pulling him in for a heartfelt embrace.

Yet Bonner the Senator would come much later. Despite a good relationship with the O'Rourkes, milking cattle and clearing land, Bonner left Woorabinda and returned to Beaudesert. He left Beaudesert, however, and found odd jobs working around Boonah – also in Southeast Queensland – milling and fencing, before moving on to Lockyer Valley, Ipswich, and then on to nearby Rosewood. Here he began jumping trains to Dalby and, knowing its illegality, adopted the pseudonym Tommy Bell, comprised of his second name and mother's maiden name.

Clearly cavalier in its use, he used his new name at a small Padua sheep station, working for three months for the McAuliffe family. Many years later this part of his past would return. In the 1970s, Mrs McAuliffe would write seeking the help of the Senator for Queensland Neville Bonner, enquiring "if he could help find out what happened to a young lad called Tommy Bell who had once worked for her husband."[38] It was "a very embarrassed Senator," noted Bonner's biographer Angela Burger, "who finally put pen to paper to acknowledge he was that Tommy Bell."[39]

It was after Padua station – in 1940 – that Bonner, this time using his actual name, attempted to enlist for World War Two. If scanning world headlines, Bonner would have read about British Prime Minister Neville Chamberlain's resignation, military strategies like the Blitzkreig, and the seismic British rescue attempt Operation Dynamo – made famous today by Hollywood director Christopher Nolan's *Dunkirk*. World War Two, touching nearly all parts of the globe, would eventually claim an astonishing 27,000 lives per day.

But the unfolding chaos didn't deter Bonner. He attempted enlistment – twice in fact – but later read in a Brisbane paper that, due to European climate, the recruitment of Indigenous Australians would cease. "I don't know how silly that sounds now," recalled Bonner in the early 1990s, "but it sounded pretty silly to us then. There had been Indigenous soldiers overseas in World War One, so we took the story with a grain of salt. But we did not get in the army."[40]

Bonner was right – there were certainly more than a handful of black diggers in World War One. In fact, two of them – Douglas Grant and Frederick Prentice – had similar stories to Bonner's. Grant – a Queenslander – was rescued from a tribal fight in the early 1900s by a passing Scottish immigrant surveyor. He was educated in Sydney, then trained as a mechanical draughtsman, and developed a passion for Shakespeare, writing and drawing. "Though Aboriginal men were excluded from military service," reads his biography on the Australian War Memorial website, "Douglas managed to enlist with the 34th Battalion in January 1916."[41] Yet he ran into the same resistance Bonner encountered decades later – "the Aborigines Protection Board intervened," reads the biography, "noting that regulations prevented Aboriginals from leaving the country without Government approval." Undeterred, Grant enlisted again, and successfully deployed with the 13th Battalion for France.

In 1957, another black World War One veteran – Frederick Prentice – was found dead and alone next to a campfire near Katherine in the Northern Territory. After some confusion it was revealed Prentice was one of a handful of black Territorian World War One veterans. Joining the Australian Imperial Force in May 1915, Prentice served in France with both the 12th and the 1st Pioneer Battalions, receiving the Military Medal for actions in Pozieres that "showed great courage, resource and ability in bringing machine guns and ammunition through the enemy barrage in the dark and broken ground."[42]

Bonner, disappointed at not being able to follow in such footsteps, returned to Woorabinda and then helped string part of a Redcliffe to Cocklebinda telephone line. World War Two had dried up Australia's labour pool and jobs were more opportune. It was then that Bonner moved to a cattle station outside of Hughenden, inland from Townsville, and began working as a stockman. He enjoyed this greatly. And here he met his first wife Mona Banfield – originally from Palm Island.

Things, however, would turn for the worse. Mona – a house servant – had slapped her white boss after an altercation, receiving a year-long expulsion to the Aboriginal settlement Palm Island. Bonner would stay on the mainland as Mona gave birth to their first son, Patrick, in 1945.

Bonner, despite his earlier years with a need for company, now seemed at this stage to enjoy some solitude. Mona returned to join Bonner but, after Patrick almost died from amoebic dysentery, he finally moved to Palm Island – a place that, in addition to his practical experiences working 'every job under the sun', would refine and solidify Bonner's philosophy. And, unknown to Bonner at the time, it would start shaping his future political career.

Palm Island

In 1895, the former slave and American educator Booker T Washington delivered his famous Atlanta Exposition Speech on race relations. In front of a white business audience, Washington reasoned with the American north – riven with strikes and labour shortages – to take on black southern workers – a third of the southern population, recently freed and more than familiar with back-breaking work.

Amid fresh wounds of the American Civil War, Washington saw an opportunity to overcome racial differences through the exchange of commerce. Notably, he implored his audience, and called on fellow blacks and other Americans, to 'cast down your bucket' – a universal and powerful metaphor for seizing what you can, where you are.

For whites, this meant looking to black labour, rather than to a growing immigrant population, to fill the needs of business and industry. And for blacks, after slavery and ongoing segregation, it meant Olympic reserves of discipline to build skills and participate in an open economy. "This was a strong conviction of Booker T Washington," notes Indigenous writer Noel Pearson, "that his people had to take responsibility so that whenever opportunities came knocking, they would be able capitalise on them. He deprecated opportunity without responsibility."[43]

I mention Washington's message here because it

runs closely to Bonner's practical philosophy of 'compromise over confrontation'. This was shaped and refined, at times sharply, during Bonner's seventeen years on Palm Island.

To say Palm Island was, in Bonner's time, a 'regimented' place to live would be correct. But labelling it a "tropical gulag" – as the Australian writer Chloe Hooper notes in *The Tall Man: Death and Life on Palm Island* – steps too far.[44] While Indigenous settlements are generally known among the Australian public, Palm Island lurched into consciousness in 2004 following the death of Cameron Doomadgee while in police custody. Riots ensued, followed by two coronial inquests, a police acquittal, and a $30 million class action civil suit.

The social chemistry that created this and other kinds of collisions is not unexpected. Steeped in tropical Queensland coastal beauty, Palm Island became an official Aboriginal settlement in 1918. Comprised largely of Indigenous Queenslanders, it has endured successive waves of Indigenous migration and, given its natural geographic seclusion, performed as an ideal isolation point. "More so than other settlements," notes one *Indigenous Law Resource*, the island "was the recipient of multiple problems because of the multiple purpose aims of the settlement as a detention centre, a training centre, an old people's home, a service centre for the infectious diseases hospital on nearby Fantome Island and a regional holding centre for the mentally ill."[45]

Multiple functions created an obvious need for order – more monarchical than hierarchical, noted one 1970 observation, and a concentration of power around the superintendent.[46] It is within this system of order that Bonner, eventually, thrived. Superintendent George Sturges proved genuine about Indigenous welfare and, taking a liking to Bonner, instituted a series of positive and constructive policies to stimulate activities and build cohesion. Bonner not only thrived under a hierarchy but proved motivated to try to create a system of black-white cohesion. As Professor Tim Rowse's commendable Senate biography of Bonner notes:

> *Though Neville was one of the few men allowed to take seasonal work on the mainland, as a canecutter around Ingham, it was on Palm Island that he was appointed a native policeman, advancing to the position of assistant works overseer with responsibility for about 300 people. Bonner was active in the Palm Island Social and Welfare Association of which he was a foundation member. On first arriving at Palm Island, Bonner had, by his own account, been 'very rebellious', but in order to get things done he became 'quite expert' in negotiating with the white authorities on the island. In 1957, convinced that discrimination could not be met by confrontation, he assisted striking Palm Island workers to draft a letter of grievance to the Director of Native Affairs in Brisbane, although some of the strikers physically attacked him for his association with the authorities.*[47]

There are three things to take from this passage. First, 'working within the system' directly corresponds with Bonner's belief in being involved in, and using, political structures and our institutions. "We have to learn to use the white man, planting the seed, playing by his rules – and beating him," he said. "It's no good trying to bring the system down or it is going to tighten up and hold firm. That's what politics is all about."[48] Second, civic participation in the Palm Island Social and Welfare Association – founded by Sturges – provided Bonner with, for the first time in his life, formal organisational and advocacy skills. In the mid-1960s, in Brisbane, he'd go on to lead the One People of Australia League and join the Liberal Party, raising his profile and elevating him to larger responsibilities. Third, we see in Bonner's story of growth – from rebel to skill builder, fixer and doer – the responsibility he advocated for in others. Bonner, indeed, 'cast down his bucket'. And the results would serve him well.

But, as Rowse alludes, it wasn't all smooth. In one incident, as settlement overseer, Bonner found himself literally in between the authorities and an angry mob following disciplinary issues around a black worker. At a tense evening standoff, settlement authorities, waiting for mainland police reinforcements, almost levelled fire at the crowd of strikers. As Bonner tried to calm the angry mob, he was descended upon. "The men lashed out with their fists until he went down," according to one account, "then began kicking him, venting their anger and frustration on the man whose rationale they could not fathom."[49] This may have killed Bonner if not for some members of the crowd, who actively shielded him from kicks and punches.

Bonner, seen as too much on the side of the authorities, would avoid such physical attacks in the future. But the rationale would stay with him for the rest of his professional life. Similar to how some black American children that study hard and read books are said to be 'acting white', Bonner was called an Uncle Tom and a 'sell out' the more he immersed himself in the mainstream political process and rose to prominence. In 1971, after entering Parliament, protestors at the newly erected Tent Embassy made clear their resentment of Bonner and his approach. An audio extract from a 2012 ABC *Hindsight* program, 'Compromise and Confrontation: Senator Neville Bonner,' features Bonner receiving an audible stream of racial taunts from the amassing protestors. Bonner, never short of eloquence, calmly responds to the astonished reporter, "If they'd have been more original, then perhaps I'd have something to worry about."[50]

Back in Queensland, the heat went beyond the usual 'Uncle Tom' rhetoric and escalated to death threats, becoming serious enough to require police investigation. As a 1971 Commonwealth Police report summarises, "Senator Bonner supports the authorities in their dealings with the aboriginal question and it is no doubt for this reason that the radical element is against him. Senator Bonner is himself an Aboriginal."[51]

While on Palm Island, Bonner would not apologise for this style of approach, and powerful people, at least by way of Indigenous affairs, had begun to notice. One figure was the Queensland Director of Native Affairs – Con O'Leary – who in 1960 offered Bonner a position as the first Aboriginal departmental officer. O'Leary's offer was for Bonner to be based in Cherbourg running an artefacts factory. Notably, he would be treated like a full staff member, which meant sharing staff quarters with white colleagues, and was highly significant at the time.

Although a great opportunity – and this was not an era for turning down opportunities – Bonner needed time to think. "You see, if I was in the staff quarters, I couldn't have other Aborigines come into the staff quarters and I couldn't have a meal up at their house," he later explained. "It was completely segregated. I said 'I couldn't live like that and neither could my wife and children'."[52]

But O'Leary needed an answer. Bonner, sitting on Palm Island with a new superintendent Barton, respectfully declined. It was a courageous decision. Bonner had grown attached to Palm Island, and the idea of not being able to see other Indigenous folk, especially his family, in his home, was too much. Over the phone, Barton played conduit, relaying the message to O'Leary. According to Bonner, here is what followed.

> So he got on the phone. We had radio telephone in those days. He got on the phone and said "Mr O'Leary, Neville Bonner has refused to come down."
>
> He said "Alright, put him on the phone."
>
> I got on the phone. He said "Well, Neville, what's your decision?"

> *I said "No, Mr O'Leary. No thank you very much. I'm honoured that you want to do that but I couldn't do it."*
>
> *He said "Well, my boy, you're either with me or against me. It appears that you're against me so put Barton back on the phone."*
>
> *So Barton got back on the phone. He said "Neville, I'm sorry. The boss says I've got to throw you off tomorrow."*
>
> *I said "What, tomorrow?"*
>
> *He said, "Yes. But he's not going to know so you can have a week."*
>
> *So I packed my gear and had a bit of a send off.*
>
> *He said "I'll give you six months start to go down, find yourself a job and a home and then I'll send the family down."*
>
> *That was in early 1960.*[53]

This would have understandably stung Bonner – an unprecedented opportunity one minute and, the next, an enemy of the Director of Native Affairs.

Yet, like all setbacks, he took it in his stride. In Brisbane, and despite his Palm Island accomplishments, Bonner defaulted to his core skill – work on a dairy farm – at Mt Crosby outside of Brisbane. Despite the sharp blow, the move would do him well, expand his opportunities and start shaping his tilt toward politics.

Island lessons, Queensland dreaming

The extent that Palm Island shaped Bonner cannot be understated. Mona and Neville had begun a family. In addition to Patrick, born 1945, a new army of young

Bonners were brought into the world – Tom (1946), Kenneth (1947), Tiny (1951), and Peter (1955). Mona and Neville even took on three foster children – Alan, Ruth and Irene – from the passing of close friends Tom and Greta Anderson. Bonner had come to Palm Island in his relatively freewheeling early twenties and now, in his mid-thirties, shouldered clear responsibilities.

Politically, however, Bonner carried island lessons with him all the way to the Senate. He knew that, even on so-called 'punishment island', a kinder term than the 'tropical gulag', Indigenous Australians may have been under a regime of control, but were nevertheless thinking for themselves. It was an imperfect 'self-determination', and Bonner maintained Indigenous Australians there – or anywhere – shouldn't be subjected to forms of guided liberty, especially from Canberra. In 1974, for example, in the Senate Chamber, criticising the then-Minister for Indigenous Affairs, Labor Senator Jim Cavanagh, he had this to say:

> *I think until he saw me he [the Minister] would not have known a blackfellow if he fell over one. He does not go around the settlements. He does not know any of the people on the settlements. I have lived on the settlements. I have relatives living on settlements and they are happy to live there. I have tried to encourage them to come out. They say: 'No. We like Palm Island. We do not want to go out. You go out and live in the rat race. We do not want to go out.'*[54]

With the same Labor scepticism, Bonner also knew what was driving Indigenous people onto settlements and places like Palm Island. Not only had Mona been sent there through overly-punitive sanction – for slapping a white woman – but measures like these, Bonner observed, were Queensland Labor-instituted policies and laws. Such laws didn't emerge from conservatives on his side of the chamber. Bonner didn't hold back:

> *The truth hurts... I can tell of some of the rotten things that happened on the Aboriginal communities under the Labor Government before the Country-Liberal Party Government came into office. If an Aborigine walked up the street and brushed a fly from his face he was put in gaol because he was supposed to have waved at the girls in the dormitory. That happened under a Labor Government. But the Country-Liberal Party Government changed all that in Queensland.*[55]

Yet a decade before he could dream of uttering these words in the federal Senate, Bonner was back on a Mt Crosby dairy farm. Work would need to be done, connections made and organisations joined if he were to climb upward in politics.

After a few years at Mt Crosby he worked at Lake Manchester with Brisbane City Council, before starting his boomerang business – 'Bonnerang' – and then working on a construction gang back at Mt Crosby building sediment basins. After a fracas with the foreman, Bonner restarted the boomerang business, creating a small factory north of Ipswich. But the second time around didn't go well. And neither did Bonner's marriage to Mona. She had return to north

Queensland and Bonner to Moreton Shire Council as a bridge carpenter.

But from here Bonner began to go from 'working man' to 'suit and tie man'. From 1968 to 1974, he led the One People of Australia League (OPAL) – an organisation formed in 1961 mainly by members of church service organisations. Mona would pass away in 1969. Bonner would meet his second wife Heather – a tireless advocate for Indigenous Australians – through OPAL. They'd first be acquaintances, then friends and then something more, eventually marrying in 1972.

They were a strong duo. Later in life, when asked what carried Bonner through his political highs and lows, he said that it was "Having the most wonderful, beautiful, human being in the world... at the other end of a telephone, and someone to come home to."[56] In 1999, as part of Bonner's Senate eulogies, the Queensland Senator and ordained Methodist Minister John Woodley spoke of the special duo they'd made:

> *When Neville Bonner became a senator, I invited him on a number of occasions to address youth groups for which I was responsible. In 1974 he came to speak to the youth group in the Sandgate parish where I was the minister. Heather and Neville came to dinner at our place before we went to meet with the youth group. I remember how delighted my small daughters were that Heather brought along—somehow or other she knew about young girls—a box of beads and other jewellery. My daughters have never forgotten that. They think Heather and Neville Bonner were the best people in all the world.*

> *But that was the sort of kindness that both Neville and Heather demonstrated so often to other people.*[57]

Heather was a highly impressive and community-minded figure. Born in 1923, she had been educated at Ipswich Girls' Grammar School and, in World War Two, joined the Australian Womens' Army Service reporting to Brisbane's Victoria Barracks. The Service fulfilled a range of important administrative, driving, signals and intelligence functions. At 18, Heather was secretary to Major General James Durant, who was in charge of Queensland's war lines of communication. Her maternal grandfather was Hugh Sinclair – a former federal Liberal Member for West Moreton. This may have explained why, with at least some understanding of the strains and commitments of public office, she'd initially been sceptical of Bonner's tilt at politics.

In 1944, Heather married an American Navy officer, which took her to the United States for thirteen years, and where she would have two sons and a daughter. Following her husband's death in a car accident, Heather eventually returned to Southeast Queensland in 1957.

Her time in the United States, specifically Washington State, taught her important lessons that she applied to her work in Indigenous affairs. "I became very interested in the plight of American Indians," she told *Women's Weekly* in 1971, "whose problems are so similar, in many ways, to those of our Aborigines."[58] After returning to Ipswich, she opened up her house to Indigenous and non-Indigenous members of the community, joining the Christian Anti-Communists Crusade and OPAL.

OPAL's goals aligned, almost perfectly, with Bonner's integrationist and 'equality agenda'. 'Assimilation' and 'integration', while similar terms on face value, have two very different meanings in Indigenous affairs. 'Assimilation' generally meant full immersion into Australian or 'white' society and relegating cultural identity, with 'integration' meaning immersion but not *entirely* leaving cultural identity at the door.

Integration, for Bonner, meant no settlements, no special legislation and no special funding. But it also meant not *entirely* disposing of culture. "I'm totally opposed to the Aboriginal race being totally and absolutely absorbed into the broader white community," he noted in the early 1990s. "I believe in integration, integrating into the broader Australian community, retaining where desired, ethnic and cultural identity, and I believe that for all people regardless of where they come from."[59] Bonner would be *the* living model of this – proud of his culture but also eager to be 'part and parcel' of the Australian community.

According to its charter, OPAL's goals were to: Endeavour to solve by influence and example, the difficulties of coloured people, firstly in the Brisbane area, and then spreading throughout the State of Queensland; attract organisations and people of repute to the ranks of the organisation; and weld the coloured and white citizens of Australia into 'One People'.[60]

These commitments created good results – or at least good *opportunities* – for both blacks and whites. "OPAL gave me the strength to survive my problems," said the Indigenous writer Rita Huggins, "and to help others who found themselves in the same boat – my own people and poor whites."[61] Huggins, taken to Cherbourg settlement from her parents as a child, worked ceaselessly for OPAL after moving to Brisbane. "OPAL was for people like me who no longer lived on the reserves and had to move into towns, and was a first step towards helping Aboriginal people," noted Huggins. "It gave white people another picture of us that they had never seen before. We had been out of sight and out of mind before that. We were decent people and this could be seen now. We were just as good as white people, but different to white people. It brought Aboriginal and non-Aboriginal people together for the first time... I began to feel like an equal."[62]

Importantly, OPAL was not part of the dominant Federal Council for the Advancement of Aborigines and Torres Strait Islanders (FCAATSI). FCAATSI, formed in the late 1950s, brought together state-based Aboriginal Advancement Leagues and pressed for greater Commonwealth government activity in Aboriginal affairs. If OPAL was about welfare, then FCAATSI was about politics. FCAATSI was "a politically and socially diverse group," according to the

National Museum of Australia: "They included peace activists, feminists, communists and Christians."[63]

FCAATSI's 'diverse group' clearly wasn't Bonner's scene – by now a staunch Christian, sceptical of protest and firmly believing Indigenous Australians be part of the Australian community. FCAATSI, in addition to supporting the 1967 referendum, borrowed and applied techniques from the sharper ends of the American civil rights movement. It wasn't just bus boycotts but the import of Black Power – including the dark shades, the goatees, the black military uniforms – and other deliberately 'extra parliamentary' methods.

Bonner would attend at least one FCAATSI meeting, flying to Canberra to participate in a national forum of over sixty Indigenous organisations. Aiming to keep a low profile – a tall order for an outspoken man – Bonner was predictably drawn into the debate. One figure grabbed the microphone and labelled him a 'black traitor' for supporting the Liberal-Country Party. But delivering one of his most searing responses, Bonner leapt to his feet, stating:

> *I am an Australian Aborigine. I came up the hard way. What I have achieved, I have achieved because I was able to stand on my two black feet. I say to heck with the rest of you. I'm going to do what I can to promote the image of my race. A man's political and religious beliefs are his own concern. If my beliefs don't accord with yours, that's just too bad.*[64]

As the 1967 referendum faded into history, the 'diverse

group' holding FCAATSI together begun to splinter and decline. Bonner's formal political career, however, was just getting started. It was becoming clear that, since his move back to Brisbane, he was cut out for politics at a significant time in Australian history. It would catapult him into a political war between a powerful conservative Queensland Premier – Joh Bjelke-Petersen – and a cosmopolitan progressive prime minister – Gough Whitlam.

But importantly, it was becoming ever clearer how a black man, from a supposedly 'backward' state, was becoming a Liberal.

Becoming a Liberal

When Bonner was asked *why* he became a Liberal, it is common to hear that it was because of Bill Hayden – former Governor-General, senior minister in the Whitlam and Hawke governments and former Leader of the Labor Party.

The story goes that, in 1967, Bonner reluctantly agreed to help some Liberal Party friends handing out how-to-vote cards for the referendum. Hayden, hopping out of a car at an Oxley polling booth, was stunned to see Bonner handing out Liberal how to vote cards. Here, according to Bonner, is the exchange that followed:

> "What are you doing handing out those how to vote cards? We do more for you bloody Aborigines that those bastards do."

> *I said "Excuse me, but who the hell are you?"*
>
> *He said "I'm Bill Hayden, I'm the Member for Oxley."*
>
> *I said "Are you?" What went through my mind was how dare someone come up to me and presume that because I was black I had to support one particular party. So I said "Look, Mr Hayden, it's like this. I'd look bloody silly handing out your cards when I'm a member of the Liberal Party."*
>
> *"Hmmph!" he said and he... walked off.*[65]

Later that day, Bonner caught up with his Liberal friends. "Give me a nomination form and I'll fill it in," he told them.[66]

This account is a favourite of mine. But it only partly explains Bonner's belief in the Liberal Party and its core principles. As I hope to have outlined so far, it discounts the journey of self-reliance and 'compromise over confrontation' Bonner had been on until this encounter with Hayden. By at least the late 1960s, he was well aware of the political atmosphere and the State Labor Government's shortfalls.

He still knew, however, that as far as assumptions went, he *should* be a Labor man. Progressive parties, after all, have dominated Indigenous and other minority support, especially since the civil rights era. Even I was surprised when first learning that Bonner was not only philosophically conservative but also a *Liberal* Senator.

In United States politics, where African Americans are virtually synonymous with the Democratic Party, this assumption is acute. "No Democratic presidential nominee has received less than 82 percent of the black vote since Kennedy's 68 percent in 1960," notes the *Washington Post*'s Ted Johnson.[67] It is generally assumed by most Americans that the Democratic Party pushed for civil rights legislation and the Republican Party did not.

It is an assumption that prevails but is entirely inaccurate. Historically, black Americans have been mainly aligned with the Republican Party, which was established in 1854 as a one-issue party – to limit and end slavery. President Abraham Lincoln – a Republican – signed the Emancipation Proclamation to free Southern slaves. This meant the first blacks, from 1863, would be able to serve in uniform. The first black US representatives on Capitol Hill were all Republicans. And it was Republicans that passed constitutional amendments ending slavery to ensure black citizenship, bestowing key constitutional rights including the right to vote. Meanwhile Democrats, from the 1860s to the 1960s, basically frustrated these Republican attempts through opposition and even acts of terror.

It is an imperfect comparison but instructive in the Australian – and Bonner's – context. For anyone who wonders *why* Bonner found his home in the conservative Liberal Party – and this was questioned incessantly in various forms – it's worth looking at the detail.

Bonner revered the Liberal Party's founder Robert Menzies. And Menzies' *Afternoon Light: Some Memories of*

Men and Events, written after Menzies' record-breaking prime ministership, offers one way to examine Bonner's beliefs. First published in 1967, in it Menzies listed five important principles that "an intelligent, free, and liberal Australian democracy shall be maintained by."[68] Menzies listed: Parliament controlling the Executive and the Law controlling all; Freedom of speech, religion, and association; Freedom of citizens to choose their own way of life, subject to the rights of others; Protecting the people against exploitation; Looking primarily to the encouragement of individual initiative and enterprise as the dynamic force of reconstruction and progress.[69]

To each of these principles Bonner was firmly aligned. First, he had cultivated a fierce respect for Parliament. In 1973, when confronted by hundreds of riled Indigenous protestors marching toward Parliament House, he pointed to the Chamber and responded, "That is Australia's Council of Elders, and you would not dare walk into an Aboriginal Council of Elders, so why should you want to march into that one?."[70] "We do not want an Aboriginal parliament," he would also famously say. "We want to be part and parcel of the Australian community. We want to see more Aborigines in this chamber."[71]

Like any legislator, he was critical of specific legislation but knew the fundamental importance of equally applying the rule of law. It provided certainty and stability, for example, when it came to property rights.

But it also meant, when deployed to its full extent, a stiff 'street level' application. He was a firm believer in capital punishment. And during the 1971 South African Springbok tour Bonner, although firmly opposed to apartheid, sided with the Queensland Premier Joh Bjelke-Petersen in supporting special legislation to prohibit protesting.

Second, Bonner had a strong Catholic faith, which overlapping with his deep cultural convictions, had a central place in his life. He held a strong respect for the views of others. His first priority, he said when going to Canberra, was to God, then nation, state and party. Queensland Presbyterians and missionaries had, like Bonner, supported assimilation and a path to education and building skills.

Third, he knew that freedom to choose one's own way of life – like he had done himself – entailed a careful balance of liberty and responsibility. It is hard to detect Bonner being cynical about those who disliked him, from activists to fellow Coalition members whispering terse things – racially motivated things – behind his back. Bonner's 'live and let live' attitude was governed by a good sense of civic responsibility, which he encouraged not simply in fellow Indigenous Australians but in *all* Australians.

Fourth, Bonner knew that protection against exploitation was achieved by building resilient and strong individuals – another of Menzies' firm beliefs. Halfway through Bonner's Senate career, he developed the *Inadmissibility of Confessions Bill*. A private member's bill, it aimed to ensure Indigenous Australians – with a limited command of English – understood their rights. The Bill dictated that a witness of standing was to be present when an Indigenous person was questioned by police relating to serious crimes. This was personal for Bonner, after his son was arrested and charged by the Queensland Police after allegedly – and strangely – begging in public. Bonner believed he'd been 'verballed' and his Bill, if enforced, would limit these instances for future Indigenous Australians.

Finally, as far as Menzies' Liberal principles went, Bonner understood that free enterprise was a lynchpin of a good economy, and that sound fiscal management created a positive commercial environment replete with opportunity. Bonner told the Senate, as a young father and labourer with the Moreton Shire Council just prior being elected to the Senate: "I would remind honourable senators on both sides of this House that until four and a half years ago I was a bridge carpenter – and proudly one – bringing home a pay packet from which I provided the then accepted every day necessities of life, admittedly with a few luxuries for a family that I had to rear," he said. "I was by no stretch of the imagination wealthy. But under a Coalition government and the stable economy which it engenderd I provided – and, I submit, provided adequately – for my family."[72]

So we know that, at least by the late 1960s, and into his

early Senate years, Bonner had found his philosophical place in the Liberal Party. But what about the practical side of politics?

In addition to a growing network and professional contact list, he also found good friends within Liberal Party ranks. Anyone who has joined a political party understands how democratising membership can be, even in larger parties. Senior ministers are accountable, in a very unique way, to their branch members who vote and have more than a say over preselection, if not policy positions. As President of OPAL, and a rising member of the party, Bonner secured $130,000 for new OPAL accommodation and offices through Liberal State Treasurer Gordon Chalk – until then the largest of any grant of its kind. It filled Bonner with immense pride, opening his eyes not just to political access but also a capacity for power, and connections, to get things done. Bonner – a growing political animal – enjoyed the deal-making and the status he was earning.

Importantly, however, he was also learning from party colleagues the substance of the policy issues. One key example was around the abolition of *The Queensland Aborigines' and Torres Strait Islanders' Affairs Act 1965* – also known as the Queensland Act. This governed Indigenous reserves and management of Indigenous people. Following the 1967 referendum, a consensus had grown that it should be repealed.

Bonner, however, strongly opposed its abolition. This put him at odds with not just Indigenous rights groups but even the then-Liberal Prime Minister John Gorton. And, while Bonner supported removing some of the clauses, his belief was down to a more thorough look at the detail. As he explained:

> *Being on the Liberal Executive, rubbing shoulders with politicians, I had learned something about the need for legislation. I understood if the 1965 Act was to be abolished, the reserves would legally no longer exist and no funds would be channelled to them. Everything would have come to a standstill. People could have starved. The land would have reverted to the Crown and they could have said to the people that they were squatting on crown land. The fact that their ancestors were here for centuries would have meant nothing.*[73]

Bonner later walked these concerns back, acknowledging this assessment at the time was slightly overstated. Indeed, in time we've seen that a fundamental problem with Indigenous communities has turned out to be the reverse of what Bonner feared – too *much* and not too little government focus.

And yet, while this position earned him some enemies at the time, it put him into alignment with figures like Bjelke-Petersen, and a range of other Country Party and Liberal figures. Philosophically, he had become a Liberal. But now it was time to run.

Taking a run at it

Bonner was unsuccessful at his first electoral attempt. He ran as third on a joint Liberal and Country Party ticket for the 21 November 1970 Senate election – an election that remains Australia's most recent Senate-only election.

The story of *how* he ended up on the ticket was interesting. He claimed his candidacy was more by 'chance' than planned, although knowing Bonner this may have been a mischievous claim. In early 1970, attending a Liberal Party Gold Coast fundraiser, he was prompted by a guest on when it would be Bonner's turn to run. Balancing a beer in one hand and cocktail plate in the other, he said he would be throwing his hat in for the Senate election later that year. Word quickly spread, followed by offers of support.

Careless with his nomination form, though, he missed the nomination deadline. But perusing the minutes of a previous Liberal Executive meeting Bonner noted the closing time wasn't clear. Asked to leave the room while the Executive deliberated, he was called back in and his nomination was accepted. Preselection, only three days later, confirmed his place at number three on the ticket.

The news of an Indigenous man on a Liberal ticket surprised many. Some felt the Country Party, by not issuing a Senate how to vote card, wasn't doing all it could to promote Bonner's candidacy.[74] Indeed, Bonner's was a political gamble in the eyes of some supporters, with some even saying they'd be voting for the ALP.

Overwhelmingly, however, Bonner benefited from good will and good people. He had help in high places

– senior federal Liberal figures including Housing Minister Dame Annabelle Rankin, Post Master General Sir Alan Hulme, National Development Minister Reginald Swartz and, importantly, Prime Minister John Gorton. Despite disagreement around the Queensland Act, to secure the support of the Prime Minister like this – as a candidate down the ballot paper – significantly raised Bonner's profile. And Gorton, intelligent and acutely aware of the political atmosphere around Indigenous issues, had time for Bonner. Bonner also secured help from OPAL. Continuing on as President, he was able to still be paid for this work and concurrently campaign as he travelled around the state. It was a good deal and Bonner desperately needed the income.

Given the Senate voting system, there was only room for five Senators. Two places would likely go to the two ahead of him on his ticket, and the other two to the ALP. The fifth position was a tough ask, given that Vince Gair was running for re-election as an independent.

Gair was an interesting and high-profile figure – Labor Premier of Queensland in the early 1950s and, after expulsion from the ALP in 1957, leading the breakaway anti-communist Democratic Labor Party. He was clearly a tactical politician and, while he and Bonner were amicable, his presence on the ballot paper only made Bonner's task more difficult.

Bonner still campaigned strongly, securing the support of people like Indigenous activist Charles

Perkins. But he also attracted what had become usual hostility from activist groups – an 'Uncle Tom', they had labelled him, or a 'sell out' and a 'token'. "The media was not kind," notes Burger. "Some of the headlines Bonner has never forgotten were, 'Liberals be kind to Aborigines week', 'Libs find new gimmick' and 'Captain Libs minstrel show'."[75]

Bonner strongly contested his alleged tokenism. "That the people on pre-selection really felt that they were using me as a gimmick, no I don't believe that," he told the journalist Robin Hughes in a 1992 interview.[76] "They were ordinary, average, decent, wonderful Australian people in the preselection. I won in on the first ballot. Now you don't win a preselection on the first ballot because you're black. You win it because people have faith in you and believe that you have the capacity to do something. I can't be persuaded otherwise."[77]

On election day, the Coalition won thirteen seats and the ALP fourteen. Despite falling short, Bonner knew this was a chance to create a profile. It had come at a huge cost financially – he had just only a dollar to his name – so he returned to his job as a bridge carpenter at the Moreton Shire Council. On a personal level, too, there was serious strain. Wife Heather displayed only lukewarm support for his candidacy and the troubles it would bring. And Bonner found campaigning, and the inevitable barbs one receives on the campaign trail, hard to take. "He was very shy," noted his ALP opponent Senator Jim Keeffe, "and I could see what an effort he was having to make. He couldn't handle the rudeness, when people cut him dead. I'd see he had a funny look on his face, but he kept on plugging away."[78]

And plug away he did. It didn't take long for his fortune to turn. Early the following year, in March 1971, Senator Dame Annabelle Rankin was appointed as High Commissioner to New Zealand, freeing up her Senate position. Bonner, likely for the first time in his life, felt entitled. Using his expanded media skills he got out in front of the story and, in political mode and hardened by experience, made as much public noise as possible, declaring he was the natural choice as next in line. Indeed, this wasn't too distant a claim – only a few months before, he had emerged as the most appropriate Liberal choice.

Party process would first need to be observed. An Executive preselection meeting was called. After a heartfelt speech reflecting on his work to advance Liberal Party principles, his pledged representation for *all* and not just a few Australians, and his assertion that a democracy's work is never complete, ensured that Bonner secured the nomination. It was 24 May 1971. News of Bonner's preselection received applause from a range of figures, from people like Charles Perkins to Joh Bjelke-Petersen. Few political figures in Australian history could capture this range of appreciation. Indeed, it was a special time.

Bonner the federalist

Bonner had arrived. Born under a tree and now an Australian Senator. The magnitude of his journey and selection to the Senate is hard to fully absorb.

Despite a successful Liberal Party preselection in May 1971, it would take a month for confirmation arrangements to be made. Bonner's official appointment took place on 15 June. As dictated by convention, he was confirmed to fill the vacancy through an exchange of letters between the Governor-General and the Governor of Queensland.

In attempting to acknowledge the significance of Australia's first Indigenous Senator, Queensland Governor Sir Alan Mansfield gently asked the Governor-General – Sir Paul Hasluck – if "Her Majesty may be pleased to recognise the fact by sending a message."[79] Hasluck's reply, channelled through his official secretary, was entirely fitting:

> I appreciate the suggestion but my reaction is that to recognise Mr Bonner as being different from any other Senator would be to accentuate racial divisions. It seems to me that the best way of honouring him is to treat him in precisely the same way as any other Senator.[80]

Bonner, however, couldn't entirely play it down. In a more light-hearted moment, he treated fellow politicians and onlookers to a 'Bonnerang' display on the Canberra Parliament House lawns. Walking into the Chamber for the first time, however, provided a more immortal moment. "As they were leading me up, I looked up and around the galleries and I could feel the whole Aboriginal race," he said, "of those who had gone before, were all up there, and I could visualise, I could hear voices and amongst those voices was the voice of my grandfather saying, 'It's alright now boy, you are finally in the council with the Australian Elders. Everything is now going to be alright'."[81]

Election to public office has been likened to finishing a marathon and then being walked over to the starting line of another. As a newly minted Senator, but with a limited formal education, Bonner would need to be prepped for the inevitable paperwork coming across his desk, an upcoming federal budget and the election slated for the following year.

Bonner's priorities upon landing in Canberra – with only five dollars in his pocket – were to God then nation, state *and* party, with Indigenous affairs woven into these personal priorities. It was an important distinction. Bonner was an Indigenous man and Senator. But he was a *Queensland* Senator. "He was always very proud of his Aboriginality," noted close friend and former Queensland Liberal Senator Ian Macdonald, "but he emphasised that he was in the Senate as a Queensland Senator and he was there to represent all of Queensland."[82]

Indeed, it was a unique state, led by a unique Premier. Bjelke-Petersen had come to power in 1968, serving until 1987, making him one of the most successful politicians in Australian history. Growing up in Southeast Queensland in the early 2000s, though, I can still recall any mention of his name in political science class would be met with a smirk or jeer. He is still seen – unfairly in my view – as a leader who, by simply fixing boundaries through gerrymandering, was able to manipulate and sustain democratic success.

But Bjelke-Petersen requires a much more careful consideration. "Country man and the conservative," wrote his biographer Hugh Lunn, Bjelke-Petersen was seen as "a winner in a state with the people often feel they are losing out. Not well educated in the full sense, he runs a state where people leave school earlier than anywhere else in Australia and where fewer places are available at University."[83]

It is an important observation – not just of the man but of the state he represented. Although known for its 'deep north' conservatism, Queensland lays claim to the first Labor government in the world (1899), in addition to the world's first general strike (1912). Even *within* state borders Queensland is a contrasting state in itself – shearers, miners and railway workers historically upon the northern frontiers with doctors, lawyers and professionals cresting the Tweed border. The state's history of free trade without the big business adds another contrast, as well as the historic Catholic versus Anglican-Presbyterian split in the legal profession, the unique rise of One Nation, and Queensland's single house of parliament.

These features have, from environmental policy to taxation, magnified comparisons with other states in the federation. Environmentalism, for example, was historically treated with some caution in Queensland, according to historian Geoffrey Bolton. "There was a tendency to see the environment movement as the creature of NSW and Victoria," he writes, "which, having achieved their own industrialisation, were now able to indulge in conscience about others."[84] Space for free enterprise – or at least minimal regulation – proved stronger in Queensland. "We did not have the strikes other states had, and we did not have a whole range of taxes which other Australians had to pay," wrote Bjelke-Petersen in his autobiography, "the idea got about that if you went to Queensland you would prosper."[85]

These themes certainly overlapped with Bonner's own ideas. While not so much 'prospering' in the modern sense of great financial wealth, he had carved out space on Queensland's difficult frontier. And, in the political realm, Bonner had been critical of Labor's management of the state when it came to Indigenous affairs, seeking instead to offer Indigenous Australians something better. After spending a decade in the Senate, he firmly believed in the rights of states to manage their own legislation without Canberra overreach. "I didn't believe that the Commonwealth had the right to interfere with State government policies," he maintained in a 1992 interview.[86] "They're two separate governments, one is a Commonwealth Government, the other is a State government... I didn't believe that there should be a confrontation between the Commonwealth Government and a State government on state legislation. I still don't believe that, that that is the correct way to do it. You negotiate and get the best deal you possibly can."[87]

This cleavage was easier to see with a Labor government – a Whitlam Government – in Canberra and Bjelke-Petersen in Brisbane. This didn't happen until December 1972 – a full year and a half after Bonner filled the Senate vacancy. But Whitlam and Bjelke-Petersen were never destined to get along. Bjelke-Petersen, wrote Lunn, "was unhappy that Whitlam had been to, and recognised, China; he regarded the severing of link with the South Vietnamese regime as a backward step; he saw Whitlam as a threat to the sovereignty of the queen; and he angrily opposed the prime minster as a socialist and a centralist wanting to sap the power of the states."[88]

Reading Hansard from this time, you can see Bonner clearly step up, taking aim and gaining confidence in his criticism of Whitlam. It wasn't just careless targeting, however, but criticism shaped by experience. One example, touched on before, was the proposed 1974 *Aboriginal and Torres Strait Islanders (Queensland Discriminatory Laws) Bill*. "The purpose of this Bill," noted Whitlam's Indigenous Affairs Minister Senator Jim Cavanagh, "is to supersede certain provisions of the laws of Queensland that discriminate against

Aborigines and Torres Strait Islanders and deny them basic human rights."[89] Bonner largely agreed with the objectives. But he notably zeroed in on a clause that read:

> *A person shall not employ an Aboriginal or Islander in Queensland (whether on a reserve or elsewhere) unless the terms and conditions of employment are not less favourable than they would be required to be if the employee were not an Aboriginal or Islander...*

"That is a very very good suggestion," Bonner noted, "but the effect of the implementation of it on the communities does worry me because I lived on a government community for a number of years." He went on to explain that, during his time on Palm Island, everyone on the settlement was paid by a fixed amount. Additional employment opportunities were created, however, by some wishing to earn extra money. "When the superintendent of the day and other members of the staff got together," said Bonner, "we worked out how much money we had and how many men we could employ. We would look at that amount of money and say: 'Is it better to pay a number of people on the community the full award according to the amount of money that we have, or should we try to employ as many as we can even though they have to be paid a little less?'." His analysis was as follows:

> *It was decided it would be far better to give a lot of people some money than to give some people a lot of money. I think that was common sense then as it is even today. I am quite sure that if the Australian*

> *Government were prepared to make available sufficient money to the authorities in Queensland so that all the people employed on the communities could be paid the award wage, then the Minister for Aboriginal Affairs and particularly the Director of Aboriginal Affairs would be only too happy to pay every person on the communities the full award wage and slightly better, that is, if they had sufficient money. But here again, I believe that in some respects the Australian Government does not live up to its responsibilities.*

I cite this example at length because it is clear there weren't many legislators, especially Senators, that could bring this sort of 'ground-level' insight to legislative debate. This is especially so today, on much broader issues, where the 'real world' experience of politicians from both major parties has narrowed.

Bonner placed this sort of practical lens over all legislation when it came to Indigenous issues. He favoured asking Indigenous people what *they* wanted – no advisory bodies, no experts, no special intermediaries. "It is of no use for the Minister to tell me that he met with some of the councillors and they told him that they want the Australian Government to take over," he said in debate. "I will not buy that one."[90] If direct consultation could be undertaken on matters much less important then why, Bonner asked, couldn't it be achieved on Indigenous issues? He noted that in Ipswich, "when a licence was to be issued for the establishment of a tavern, a hotel or something or other, all the people in the community were given the opportunity of voting to say whether they wanted that tavern opened in their community or not. This can be done for people in Ipswich and for people in Brisbane but it cannot be done for the Aboriginal people in the communities."[91]

Bonner was conscious, however, that all the intense focus on Indigenous affairs, especially at a legislative level, was raising expectations of government. And he was concerned about social cohesion. In May 1975, almost a decade since the landmark 1967 referendum, he said this in the Chamber:

I am a little concerned because many young Aboriginal people in the community today have become impatient for change. They have become angry young men and angry young women. We have had examples of this in demonstrations against the Department of Aboriginal Affairs. I refer to demonstrations in George Street, Brisbane, and in Canberra, against the previous Government and against the present Government... Because of past discrimination and things that have happened in the past, a group of young Aboriginal men and women could become angry, and outside this place they could shout, 'Down with the whitey', or something about some race of people.[92]

It was a valid concern. Yet while Bonner uttered these words in the Chamber, it wouldn't matter. At least initially. Bigger issues were at play.

Untold pressures – the 1975 dismissal

Gough Whitlam's dismissal as prime minister – on 11 November 1975 – happened toward the middle of Bonner's Senate career. As Australia's most destabilising political crisis, at least since federation, the event placed significant pressures on Bonner.

As we know, Bonner held a towering respect for Australia's established institutions and the British Monarchy. At the 1998 Constitutional Convention, a year prior to his death, he played a key role in the 'No' campaign against the republic. "How dare you," he famously scolded the Convention on the third day. "You told my people that your system was best. We have come to accept that. We have come to believe that. The dispossessed, despised adapted to your system. Now you say that you were wrong and that we were wrong to believe you."[93] This part of his speech was sharp, and clearly well-remembered. But in other parts he spoke delicately on the rule of law, the Westminster system, judicial impartiality and, importantly, "that Government House must also be a political-free zone."[94]

Bonner was clearly unhappy – but not cynical – about the republican design. I sense he was more saddened that, after his lifetime encouraging integration and assimilation to such high ideals, the goal posts were moving once again. "Republicanism is a vote of no confidence in the existing system," he closed out by saying, "but you forget that you have taught us to love, honour and respect that system."[95]

Like all of Bonner's public utterances, it wasn't just academic – he was speaking from some experience of 'the system', especially when it came to the awesome reserve powers of the governor-general. In 1975, only a few years into his Senate career, he struck momentum in levelling criticisms at the Whitlam Government. Whitlam clearly started well – promising 'It's time' and fresh themes of change – but from inflation to employment things were unravelling.

In September of that year, Bjelke-Petersen punctured Whitlam's Senate hopes by filling a Queensland Senate Vacancy with the Labor Party member – but anti-Whitlam – Albert Patrick 'Pat' Field. Rather than fill the vacancy with the Labor Party's preferred candidate, which tended to follow convention, Bjelke-Petersen asked the Labor Party to produce a list of three names that he could choose from.

Bonner, with other Queensland Liberals, wasn't entirely happy with the approach. "I entered the Senate in similar circumstances," he noted, "and no one then asked the Liberal Party to submit a panel of names to parliament."[96]

But another more damaging issue – less to do with political manoeuvring and more to do with Whitlam mismanagement – was playing out. In May 1975, it emerged that Whitlam attempted to seek Commonwealth funding through Pakistani banker Tirath Khemlani. It was a step too far for Malcolm Fraser, who promised to keep the Whitlam Government on fiscal life support if Whitlam could steer clear of 'reprehensible and extraordinary events'. The 'loans affair', as it came to be known, violated the commitment, ultimately creating a situation where Whitlam was unable to pass supply – what Americans call a 'government shut down'.

Coming into November 1975 things, clearly, were desperate. All Whitlam and his government needed, indeed *all* that the Australian Government needed, was for two Senators to cross the floor to continue supply – two Senators with an independent enough mind. It was here that Bonner's name emerged, along with fellow Liberals Alan Missen and Eric Bessell.

Determining precisely *why* Bonner's name had arisen is interesting to consider. Had it been a few years later, after he'd become more independent and outspoken, then it would've made sense. But I sense that, at this stage of Bonner's Senate career, only three years in, it had more to do with the *kind* of person Bonner was – not his politics. Bonner was clearly a 'people person' – as we'd now call him – enjoying strong relations with a range of parliamentarians. Whitlam himself had taken time to seek out Bonner, offering congratulations after Bonner's first Senate appearance. In the Parliamentary Bar, Bonner often had to buy the first round and evade additional shouts – becoming known as the 'one beer Senator' – not only to set a good example but because he was clearly good company. Even in 1983, prior to the March election when it was clear Bonner was to lose his Senate position, Bob Hawke phoned offering that, if required, something could be arranged.

Considered a deliberative and reasonable man, Bonner was clearly well-liked across the political constellation – amicable enough to at least help a desperate government. Indeed, this all weighed heavily on Bonner – the pressure of all those pensions, he thought, and other critical payments, not getting to people in need. As Bonner's biographer Angela Burger wrote, the events "were to cause Bonner such agonies of mind, the trauma of decision over a long twenty-six days, that they were to have an effect he cannot shake off."[97] It had shown the sharp change in Bonner's life – only five years before a council bridge carpenter for a local council but, now, feeling the weight of an entire administration and federal budget on his shoulders.

The pressure, however, finally eased as Government House – that usually 'politics free zone' – made the decision to dismiss Whitlam. The Governor-General, Sir John Kerr, installed Fraser as caretaker Prime Minister and a full election was called for 13 December 1975. The Coalition won overwhelming majorities in both houses.

Reflecting on the events, Bonner said:

> *I was relieved the decision had been taken out of my hands. I am not proud of it, but I was relieved for the*

> *well-being of the nation. Kerr must have been a psychic. For whatever reason he moved when he did, I would say it was from the best of motives because he was afraid of bloodshed – either that or he knew there were enough of us in the Senate not to let that happen.*[98]

The events of 1975 only enhanced, rather than undermined, Bonner's respect for Australia's constitutional furniture. The event also built his confidence and set the scene for the balance of his time in Parliament.

'As low as anyone can get'

When Malcolm Fraser passed away in 2015, his principal achievements as prime minister were seen as the creation of the Special Broadcasting Service (SBS), providing needed safety for additional Vietnamese refugees, enhancing greater protection for the Great Barrier Reef and delivering self-government to the Northern Territory.

Northern Territory independence, and the *Aboriginal Land Rights (Northern Territory) Bill 1976*, served as a critical moment in Bonner's Indigenous advocacy. Initiated by Whitlam, the Bill was carried through by Fraser and, importantly, supported by Bonner. "I am proud to say that the Government places a great deal of importance on what this Bill means to my people," he told the Chamber, "and intends to keep faith with them."[99]

Notably, he saw the Bill through a broader package of "compensation for dispossession", not just for Indigenous Australians in the Northern Territory but across Australia. "This nation has to answer that question some day," he said, "and the sooner the better."[100]

Indeed, the term 'compensation' understandably wobbled some in the Liberal Party, and here Bonner was encouraged to trim his sails with more guided language. He ultimately envisaged this compensation to fund a statutory body – similar to the ABC – to regiment a series of programmes for Indigenous welfare across a range of areas.

But a closer reading of Bonner's use of the term, and the Bill itself, shows less about dollar-for-dollar 'handouts' but rather underlines his 'equality agenda' and idea of Indigenous self-determination, modern capital and land rights – recognition for what one owns and then parking aside funds to be able to be used for investment. The Act created Aboriginal Land Councils and Aboriginal Trusts for this purpose.

Bonner's outspokenness, however, was becoming emblematic of a principled Senator with an 'independent' – and sometimes seemingly stubborn – mind. He clashed with Fraser, crossing the floor thirty-four times and went multiple rounds with Bjelke-Petersen. Granted, not all floor-crossings were under Fraser, with whom he appeared in lock step on Indigenous issues, and he had also enjoyed an amicable start with Bjelke-Petersen. But Bonner found a significant amount to contest as a Senator towards the end of the 1970s.

In early 1976, Bonner joined other Liberal Senators in voting against Fraser's social security bill because it removed a funeral benefit for pensioners. In the same year, an austerity budget saw Bonner go into bat for the Methodist Church and Salvation Army in Queensland. Here, again, he clashed with Fraser but was able to get some funding restored.

Following Whitlam's 1975 dismissal, the Fraser Government in 1977 also reactivated a referendum to allow for simultaneous elections between the House of Representatives and the Senate. Whitlam had previously proposed it in 1974 and the Liberals had apposed it at that time. Now, however, the Liberals were seeking to make the same changes. When opportunities arose, on television and at speaking events, Bonner recycled old talking points, pointing out the contradiction and his belief that the Senate should retain its autonomy as a house of review.

It wasn't only on domestic issues that Bonner bumped heads. He also clashed with Fraser and Foreign Affairs Minister Andrew Peacock over East Timorese independence. He heavily criticised what he deemed as their inactivity, even recording a radio broadcast that was transmitted – illegally – to Timorese Fretilin leaders.

On Indigenous issues more broadly he felt his talents were not fully being called upon, given his cultural intermediary skills and the practical knowledge that he could bring to Indigenous issues. Although made chair of a Joint Select Committee on the adequacy of Indigenous Northern Territory laws, he was later left out of critical discussions between Fraser and the Indigenous Affairs Minister Ian Viner. Bonner predicted – I'd say correctly – that his outspokenness was doing him little favours. But he still remained a collegial Liberal team player, making this observation after Viner's visit to Queensland's top end:

> *I have never seen a non-Aboriginal person, in such a short time, be able to communicate with and gain the confidence of a group of Aboriginal people. I do not believe it probable that I will ever see it happen again.*[101]

Indeed, it was a glowing endorsement for Viner, or any Minister, in a difficult portfolio at a difficult time. Bonner would pay great homage to other Senators and their work over the years in Indigenous affairs – Viner, Fred Chaney, Peter Rae, Peter Baume, Philip Lynch, Margaret Guilfoyle and Bernie Kilgariff all scored highly in Bonner's view.

As many problems as Bonner appeared to have within his own Liberal administration, however, it was growing smaller in comparison to the problems he would encounter with Bjelke-Petersen. To be a clear proponent of States' rights – which Bonner was – didn't mean staying silent on what he assessed as bad ideas around local government and health services.

In 1978, Bonner notably clashed with Bjelke-Petersen and the Queensland Indigenous Affairs Minister and Liberal – Charles Porter – over their decision to take over control of the Mornington Island and Aurukun Reserves. Although tempting to categorise the clash as over 'land rights', "it wasn't actually a land rights issue at that time," Bonner explained.[102] With strong local support, Aurukun was run by the Presbyterian Church. "The Queensland Government decided that the church wasn't doing its job," Bonner noted, "so they decided that they would take over the community and in plain English they sacked all of the church leaders." Bonner's involvement, he said, was "because I believed that they were right. They had a right to remain as a Christian community if they so desired. I didn't believe the Queensland Government had any right at all to take the action that they did, and I fought them all the way."[103]

'All the way' meant, should it arise, departing the Liberal Party. After a fiery television clash with Porter – notably a fellow Liberal and not a Country Party member – he'd made this position more than clear. Afterward Bonner said:

> ... that in due of some of the statements that were made, I would have to consider my position within the Liberal Party. In other words, I was inferring that unless something better came out of the negotiations between the Commonwealth, the State and the people of Aurukun, I would probably sit on the cross-benches. It didn't pan out that way, there was a bit of compromising going on

> *on all sides of the field, I rethought my position, and felt it was better that I stayed in parliament because I could do more there and it would be a waste of time my getting out and letting the position go.*[104]

The Aurukun and Mornington Island issue had clearly pushed Bonner to the brink. But it came in second to Bjelke-Petersen's pressure to defer a federal trachoma survey in Queensland Indigenous communities. Bjelke-Petersen had believed two members of the survey team were actively campaigning for the Labor Party while undertaking their work. "To me," said Bonner, "stopping that trachoma survey was the worst thing he has ever done. It was made worse because it was done for purely political reasons. I think that's as low as anyone can get."[105]

At around this time, Bonner was hitting lows himself. On a fact finding visit to Canada, after making a point of not meeting any Indigenous Canadians as part of the official programme, he earned a censure motion from the Canadian Parliament. As well as his cultural curiosity, he was eager to see how Indigenous Canadians had been integrated into mainstream society. Bonner was a good media performer but not an international diplomat. Closer to home, while on a family holiday, he was denied a beer at a Mt Isa pub. "We don't serve darkies," he was told.[106]

The severe indignity, compounded by mounting political problems toward the end of the 1970s, would've clearly destabilised his enthusiasm for 'compromise over confrontation'. But he capped off 1979 with some silver lining – being awarded the Australian of the Year. He also received life membership from the Young Liberals – an exclusive award on its own but even rarer for a sitting politician.

In sum, however, the political tug of war between Brisbane and Canberra appeared to be taking a toll. For a federal politician, this was where it mattered the most – from within his own party. His notable independence had apparently created a grass roots concern within local branches and other rank and file members. Importantly, however, this was not on a "racial basis" according to one key Liberal figure at the time. "It was suggested that Neville had been taking things for granted and not courting the branches as all incumbents need to do to retain support," this private observer notes.[107] "There was an impression of general complacency, not just by Neville but by other party leaders, who didn't make it clear to branches how much a lower ranking on the senate ticket would harm his chances."[108]

In the lead up to the 1983 federal election Bonner was relegated to third on the Senate ticket – a virtually unwinnable position. Fraser noted it was one of his deepest regrets as prime minister. In a 2000 speech at Old Parliament House, John Howard labelled it one of the Queensland Liberal Party's "more ignoble pre-selection decisions."[109]

Both Fraser and Howard's observations point to a

certain 'tone deafness' within the Queensland Liberal Party at the time and, as some may argue, that still exists today. It was, and remains, a source of great esteem that the first Indigenous parliamentarian was a devoted Liberal and served at the highest level of national political representation for over a decade. It presented encouragement for current and prospective members and, in raw political terms, offered tactical gain and electoral appeal. Liberal Senator Ian Macdonald, a close friend, for example, spoke of Bonner's inspiring choice to be a member of the Liberal Party:

> *I was always so proud that Neville Bonner was a Liberal—and, to a degree, it reinforced my commitment to the Liberal Party as a party for all people. I was ever so proud of the party when Neville Bonner came to be elected as Australia's first Aboriginal parliamentarian. He always used to emphasise in those early days—and I was only a bit of a kid then—that he was 'a Senator for all Queenslanders'.*[110]

At the 1983 federal election Bonner would win 105,000 votes in his own right as an Independent – a stunning outcome. Yet Bonner's relegation effectively cancelled out these appeals. The need to promote, manage and nurture good candidates and even sitting members will always be in competition with the ruthlessness of merit, ambition and numbers – all key considerations in party politics.

Labor, it seems, understood this. Peter Beattie – as Queensland ALP Secretary in the early 1980s – not only offered Bonner ALP preferences when Bonner officially chose to run as an Independent a month prior to the 1983 election. The ALP also instantly offered him a position at the ABC board following his defeat. Nothing was as forthcoming from the Liberal Party.

And while Beattie's promise never emerged, and Beattie never explained why, the broad lesson is clear – Bonner was a remarkable Australian, by March 1983, with significant talent. His departure from the Liberal Party was wrenching.

This became even more acute by the tactical errors adopted by some in the Liberal Party at the time. Kathryn Sullivan (nee Martin) – who emerged as number one on the Liberal Senate ticket – commendably offered to relegate herself down the order in favour of seniority following the 1983 Liberal preselection process. This would mean Bonner would be listed first, followed by Sullivan and then David MacGibbon. But this proposal was immediately knocked back by the Party Executive – "the power brokers on the hill," to use Bonner's words at the time.[111]

Compounding this again was the fact that, in the following year, Sullivan moved to the House of Representatives, running successfully for the new Southeast Queensland seat of Moncrieff and serving until 2001. Sullivan, notably, was very personally close to Bonner and had been since the late 1960s – "He was my friend, my mentor and my black dad, and to this day I grieve his passing from the Australian parliament,"[112] she told the House of Representatives when retiring in 2001 (Bonner passed away in 1999). The "very best thing that ever happened in my political life was coming in here with him," she added. "He was the greatest Australian I have ever known."[113]

As bitter as this episode was, especially coming from within his own ranks, it wouldn't sour Bonner or his relations within the Liberal Party. In the same speech, given in honour of Bonner's legacy, Howard also had this to say:

> ... there was a period of very significant and lengthy estrangement from the Liberal Party. He was badly treated and as time went by many people came to recognise that. And one of the more emotional moments I've had as prime minister was to confer upon him life membership of the Queensland Division of the party when he rejoined it in 1996 and to embrace Neville both physically and metaphorically back into the Liberal fold at the State Convention on that occasion. It was a special moment for us because it was something that had to be put right. And it was put right and he showed an enormous grace and generosity of spirit in the way in which he responded.[114]

Post-Senate career

Bonner's electoral loss was a blow. He was clearly dejected. But he had lived a life of setbacks and it was also a time for new horizons.

With nationwide ten percent unemployment the newly elected prime minister, Bob Hawke, promised to fix the economy and get Australians back into jobs. This even included a role for Bonner, with a position on the ABC Board. He was thus given a place at the table with a list of other high-profile Australians.

Bonner, now living in Ipswich, filled in his time launching books, opening galleries, serving on the Old Parliament House advisory committee, and as an official visitor to Queensland's prisons. Although unpaid, he was grateful. "I do it because I feel that I'm making a contribution in one form or another," he said. "So, I'm kept fairly busy. I thank God for that. I couldn't think of anything worse than retiring and just sitting and wasting away."[115] He also took up something that many people say, surprisingly, gives them a sense of relief – playing golf.

How did he look back on his time in the Senate? "I spoke as an ordinary, average Australia, albeit Aborigine," he said.[116] "Forget Neville Bonner as the person, the major thing was that for the first time in history, an indigenous person had made it into the federal parliament where all laws pertaining to this nation are made. And I had to be able to stand up and debate the issues concerning the nation as a whole, and I think I did reasonably well."[117]

Issues 'covering the nation as a whole' is an important distinction. I sense it has been a mistake, as some have done, to look at Bonner's legacy purely through the prism of Indigenous advocacy – as an Indigenous *only* Senator – and as "pleasing nobody."[118] Looking at things 'as a whole' broadens the focus of his time in the Senate, crystallising the sheer latitude of the issues he helped troubleshoot, and reminds us that, like all politicians, he had a range of interests to uphold. Aurukun and Mornington Island, he noted, were not 'land rights' issues but issues around local government and representation. A sea of black advisory and intermediary bodies, too, he said, was no match for the body that represented all Australians – the parliament. His 'equality agenda' focused on no settlements, no special legislation and no special funding, aiming to eventually put black and white on the same equal page. And a humming economy, stewarded by sound fiscal management, benefited all Australians, and not just black or white. Bonner fundamentally tried to bring black and white together as he had since the days of OPAL.

His life in Ipswich, in fact the street on which he lived, he noted, was a place where people took very slim notice of complexion. It was a sense of community that he was proud to be a part of – miles away from his difficult start and that tough first day at school.

Unlike many other Australian political figures, he didn't fade into society but, given his distinctive achievements and appearance, maintained a public profile. Indeed, he had a hard time convincing people that he *wasn't* a Senator anymore.

As the only full time ABC Board member, he was often sent to the more remote parts of Australia. Here Bonner told of one amusing instance:

> *I once did a tour with the Managing Director of the ABC, David Hill. When he got back, he said to his colleague, 'I'll never travel again with that so and so.'*
>
> *They said, 'Why?'*
>
> *He said, 'Everybody knows him. You can't walk down a street without someone pulling you up and wanting to talk to him.'*

But with characteristic modesty he quickly qualified:

> *I don't say that in a nasty prideful way. I say it with a great deal of pride because that's Australia.*[119]

Testament to a great man

Few funerals, noted former Queensland National Senator Ron Boswell, can be described as "spectacular Party". But Bonner's state funeral, held in Ipswich, "was a spectacular funeral."[120]

Bonner passed away at 77 years of age due to respiratory illness. Mitchell Kunde, Bonner's grandson delivered the eulogy, noting the final months of a man of great charisma:

> *A few months ago, I accompanied my grandfather on his last official engagement to the men's reconciliation committee dinner in Brisbane. Grandfather was presented with an award in honour of his outstanding contribution to the process of reconciliation. When he announced that to be his public swan song, all 550 men, without exception, rose to their feet and gave a deafening*

acclamation, many with tears in their eyes.

It has been said that Neville Bonner was a role-model and an example to Aboriginal people, but, by the way he lived his professional and family life, he should be an inspiration to all people. And today I pray that every Australian will learn the spirit of togetherness from the life of this remarkable man – a genuine Australian legend – my grandfather.[121]

The range of condolences in the Senate Chamber the following week spoke to the breadth of Bonner's appeal. But it is also interesting to see how each Senator captured a special and unique part of Bonner. Senator Robert Hill, for example, spoke of the cultural balance that Bonner exemplified to both black and white Australians:

To Aboriginal people he said: be proud of your heritage, Aboriginality, language, culture, values and spiritual knowledge; recognise the special capacity of Aboriginal people to enrich the total Australian society; do not accept that you are of necessity disenfranchised within that broader society; you are entitled to full opportunities and benefits of that society and the responsibilities which come with that opportunity; accept the personal effort which will be necessary to achieve your full potential; and it will not be easy, as Neville personally demonstrated.

To non-Aboriginal Australians he urged the mirror image: appreciate the unique history of Aboriginal Australia; recognise that embracing Aboriginal heritage will enrich Australia; appreciate the disadvantage suffered by continuing generations of Aboriginal

> *Australians arising out of dispossession not just of the land but of a way of life and the responsibility that flows to help overcome that disadvantage; and accept the legitimacy of Aboriginal people to the broader aspirations of all Australians.*[122]

Opposition Senator John Faulkner, speaking of Bonner's 1983 electoral loss, noted Bonner's advocacy both in and out of the Senate:

> *Australia at that time lost a fine representative from the parliament but, after leaving politics, he continued to fight for the equality of indigenous people and respect for Aboriginal culture, and I think it is fair to say that, in Neville Bonner, here was a man who was an inspiration for very many Australians. On behalf of the opposition, I join with the government in expressing our sincere condolences on his death and our sincere sympathy to his wife, family and friends.*[123]

Senator Macdonald also recorded an amusing story from a trip Bonner made up to Innisfail and stumbled into the wrong meeting room – an Apex Club Convention. However, it didn't seem to matter:

> *In the middle of whatever we were discussing, the Apexians stood as a person and applauded him so warmly. He got to the top of the table and sat down. The chairman of the meeting looked at him and he looked back. The chairman eventually got up and whispered to him and it became obvious that Neville Bonner had come in, quite uninvited, to the wrong room in this centre.*
>
> *Never to be outdone, Neville, with a bit of encouragement from the audience who started clapping him when that was explained, got up and gave a 10-minute off-the-cuff*

> *address about his role and the role that service clubs played. It was a warm experience for both the Apexians and, I think, for Neville Bonner, that he was so well-regarded and such a significant figure that he was able to get away with what would, for other people, have been an embarrassment.*[124]

Other Senators would note Bonner's fierce respect for institutions, his vital absence of pretension and that he "was a man you could not but like."[125] Indeed, in putting these pages together, I have heard nothing but strong praise for Bonner – a great Queenslander and a great Australian.

What can Bonner teach us?

The British MP and historian Kwasi Kwarteng writes that "It is no use taking 2014, 2010 or 1990 assumptions and then trying to read them back into a time before the First World War."[126]

In assessing Bonner's contemporary legacy, I feel similarly cautious for fear of doing the same in reverse – transferring too much from the past onto the present. Clearly, so much has changed since the era in which Bonner grew up. But in Bonner's personal and professional life, we can continue to find timeless lessons, from good behaviours worth emulating to the importance of a genuine community.

The most immediate lesson from Bonner is clearly resilience. Having an entire primary school leave because of your complexion, or being racially abused for asking for milk, would've been intensely scarring to deal with as a boy. Even as a grown man, with a family to feed, he'd show up to jobs that had mysteriously disappeared, revisiting the indignity he faced in earlier years.

But despite these ongoing setbacks, continuing to work 'every job under the sun', and with little money in his pocket, he seemed to not only survive but thrive. He learnt the art of climbing a hierarchy which, importantly, is not an endorsement of 'the system' but playing the 'rules of the game'. And, like many others who learn and use these rules, it had served him well. "If I achieved goal after goal then perhaps so can you in this easier and more enlightened era for Aborigines and Torres Strait Islanders," he told a Griffith University audience when receiving an Honorary Doctorate in 1993.[127]

We also see in Bonner an avoidance of resentment. This is a timeless and positive trait, even according to Aristotle, who notes that the great man "does not bear grudges, for it is not a mark of greatness of soul to recall things against people, especially the wrongs they have done you, but rather to overlook them."[128] Bonner showed, like all great Australians, that to avoid grudges and overlook wrongs is not some far off Aristotelian virtue but an admirable goal within reach for all of us. When grandson Mitchell Kunde spoke of Bonner as 'a genuine Australian legend', he may not have been thinking of Aristotle but instead tapped our common Australian belief in optimism under stress and in the face of great uncertainty.

To avoid resentment also requires empathy. Bonner's maiden speech had placed a premium on looking after those less fortunate. Importantly, Bonner stayed grounded, despite reaching national fame and spending over a decade in the federal parliamentary chamber. It is hard to say that this wasn't, on a very personal level, driven overwhelmingly by his faith. "Don't look down upon one of God's children," he said, "because you'll answer in time to come."[129]

Empathy also guided his respect for those not on the same side of politics. He clearly faced heat from the protest movement of his era. But he notably still had time for those that didn't always have time for him, whether he was brokering a deal between Tent Embassy protesters and Prime Minister McMahon, or much later corralling civil society activists to take a stand against the Queensland Government's takeover of Aurukun and Mornington Island. To get praise from someone like Charles Perkins, which Bonner received on multiple occasions, and despite being a Liberal conservative, illustrated a significant and unusual appeal.

It's then unsurprising that the sum of these traits – resilience, minimal resentment, empathy – underpinned Bonner's belief in genuinely working together, through established institutions, rather than creating new ones or any sense of separatism. In one of his sharper observations, he labelled Whitlam's national Aboriginal consultative council as "auto-apartheid", adding that it'd be "ludicrous... to suggest that there will be an Aboriginal parliament within Australia."[130] With proposals to create an Indigenous Parliament, this assessment is again highly relevant today.

I sense Bonner found much more time for the belief that reconciliation – now a loaded term in Indigenous politics – was to be found among individuals rather than through national institutions. And on the much milder question of getting more Indigenous Australians into politics, he'd say there was no special formula other than what worked for other Australians – educating one's self on the issues and being more politically aware.[131]

When it came to formal politics, there was one key lesson that still holds so much currency in our times – how you look shouldn't determine how you vote. It is a simplistic point. But one that needs constant revisiting, and where to be black – or any minority – on the conservative side of politics remains to be seen as 'selling out'. Even today, when formal political allegiances are shifting, it's easily forgotten what being an individual *actually* constitutes, and the underlying principles of liberty, choice and freedom that support this idea. Indeed, Bonner was *the* example of Menzies' statement that "the real freedoms are to worship, to think, to speak, to choose, to be ambitious, to be independent, to be industrious, to acquire skill, to seek reward. These are the real freedoms, for these are of the essence of the nature of man."[132]

In everyday terms, Bonner's espousal of his 'real freedoms' could at times clearly land him in hot water. On the surface it lent an incoherence to Bonner's time in the Senate. But, as I hope to have made at least partly clear, he was better understood as a pragmatic federalist, even a localist, standing up for the State of Queensland while also being committed to *real* equality for Indigenous Australians. His integrationist and 'equality agenda' – no settlements, no special legislation and no special funding – ironically remains both distant and achieved, with government continuing to dominate the lives of some Indigenous Australians but with many others also healthily sceptical of a culture of 'hand outs' versus 'hand ups'.

Despite needing to run as Independent at the 1983 federal election all, eventually, was forgiven with the Liberal Party. Political parties require party discipline. But they also require independent thinkers. Bonner's independent thinking over-ruled party considerations.

Finally, Bonner's life is a lesson in the importance of community. As many doors would close there would be others that would open. And this was down to good people, whether it was a chance to attend school – albeit briefly – or the offer of a job on the city waterworks at Mt Crosby. Ahead of Bonner's final election, he noted receiving an envelope from an eighty-three year old lady who "put a $2 note in the letter and spent half a page of apologising because that's all she could afford."[133] Indeed, in every quarter, whether supportive friends in the Liberal Party, his mother and Grandmother doing their best to get him off to a good start, or the support of wife Heather, Bonner benefitted from having decent people in his life – those that cared for him and those that could get him through.

It's a nice reminder, amid modern rootlessness and our fraying social connections, of the responsibilities we all possess. Like Bonner, we would do well to not only look after our communities but look after ourselves too.

Endnotes

1. Neville Bonner, "First Aboriginal in the Australian federal parliament: Interview with Robin Hughes," *Australian Biography*, 13 January, 1992, http://www.australianbiography.gov.au/.
2. Ibid.
3. Ibid.
4. Ibid.
5. Tony Blair, *A Journey*, Hutchinson, London, 2010, p. vx.
6. Ibid.
7. Greg Lukianoff and Jonathan Haidt, "The Coddling of the American Mind," *The Atlantic*, September 2015, https://www.theatlantic.com/magazine/archive/2015/09/the-coddling-of-the-american-mind/399356/.
8. Bonner, "First Aboriginal in the Australian federal parliament: Interview with Robin Hughes."
9. Angela Burger, *Bonner: A Biography*, Macmillan, Melbourne, 1979, p. 3.
10. Ibid., p. 5.
11. Ibid., p. 8.
12. Ibid., p. 5.
13. "Liberals worried by Aboriginal," *Canberra Times*, 10 April 1971.
14. Senator Neville Bonner, *Commonwealth Parliamentary Debates*, Senate, 7 June 1973, p. 2479.
15. Robert Hughes, *The Fatal Shore: The Epic of Australia's Founding*, Vintage, London, 2003, p. 48.
16. Although Bonner cites 20,000 years in Hansard, the more correct figure is 60,000 years. Bonner is likely citing the ashes found from a human cremation in the Murray Basin in 1968. See Geoffrey Blainey, *A Shorter History of Australia*, William Heinemann Australia, Melbourne, 1994, p. 218.
17. Brian Whimborne, "Historical Reality and Australian Identi-

ty," *Quadrant*, January-February 2013, p. 52.

[18] Senator Neville Bonner, *Commonwealth Parliamentary Debates*, Senate, 8 September, 1971, p. 553.

[19] Geoffrey Bolton, *Spoils and Spoilers: A History of Australians Shaping their Environment*, Allen & Unwin, Sydney, 1981, p. 9.

[20] "Neville Bonner: His early life and his role as a Senator," Interviewed by Robyn Buchanan, 1995.

[21] Burger, *Bonner*, p. 63.

[22] Ibid., p. 3.

[23] Shelby Steele, *The Content of Our Character: A New Vision of Race in America*, Harper Perennial, New York, 1998, p. 59.

[24] Gough Whitlam (ALP Leader), *1972 Election Campaign Launch*, Blacktown, 13 November 1972, https://electionspeeches.moadoph.gov.au/speeches/1972-gough-whitlam.

[25] Mike Bruce, "Why the university system is failing our graduates," *The New Daily*, 22 October 2019, https://thenewdaily.com.au/finance/work/2019/10/22/australian-university-graduate-jobs/.

[26] David Gillespie, *Free Schools*, Macmillan, Sydney, 2014, p. 43.

[27] Senator Neville Bonner, *Commonwealth Parliamentary Debates*, Senate, 7 March 1974, p. 181.

[28] Ibid.

[29] "Bonner", Interviewed by Robyn Buchanan.

[30] Ibid.

[31] Senator Neville Bonner, *Commonwealth Parliamentary Debates*, Senate, 5 May 1976, p. 1552.

[32] Fred Chaney quoted in Noel Pearson, *Radical Hope*, Black Inc, Collingwood, 2011, p. 182.

[33] Amity Shlaes, *Coolidge*, Harper Perennial, New York, 2014, p. 8.

[34] Christopher Zinn, "Neville Bonner obituary" *The Guardian*, 15 February 1999, https://www.theguardian.com/news/1999/feb/15/guardianobituaries2.

35. Rohan Sullivan, "Bonner, Neville (1922–1999)" *Associated Press*, 5 February 1999, http://oa.anu.edu.au/obituary/bonner-neville-28098/text35812; Mitch Ziems, "Neville Bonner: Voice of a broken people" *The 8 Percent*, 26 May 2016, https://the8percent.com/neville-bonner-voice-of-a-broken-people/.
36. Edward Palmer, *Early Days in North Queensland*, Project Gutenberg, October 2012, http://gutenberg.net.au/ebooks09/0901071h.html.
37. Burger, *Bonner*, p. 18.
38. Ibid., p. 19.
39. Ibid., p. 20.
40. Ibid.
41. "Douglas Grant," Australian War Memorial, https://www.awm.gov.au/learn/schools/resources/anzac-diversity/aboriginal-anzacs/douglas-grant.
42. Territory Studies, https://www.territorystories.nt.gov.au/handle/10070/226615?mode=simple.
43. Noel Pearson, "White guilt, victimhood and the quest for a radical centre," *Griffith Review*, No 16, Winter 2007, https://www.griffithreview.com/articles/white-guilt-victimhood-and-the-quest-for-a-radical-centre/.
44. Chloe Hooper, *The Tall Man*, Hamish Hamilton, Camberwell, Victoria, 2008, p. 11.
45. Elliott Johnston, "Aboriginal deaths in custody - Royal Commission, Reports - Inquiry into the death of Johnson, B.M.," Australian Parliament House, 17 April 1990, https://parlinfo.aph.gov.au/parlInfo/search/display/display.w3p;query=Id:%22publications/tabledpapers/HPP032016010387%22;srcl=sml.
46. JPM Long in Ibid.
47. Tim Rowse, "Bonner, Neville Thomas (1922–1999)," Biographical Dictionary of the Australian Senate, http://biography.senate.gov.au/bonner-neville-thomas/.
48. Burger, *Bonner*, p. 31.

[49] Ibid., pp. 32-33.

[50] ABC Hindsight, "Compromise and Confrontation: Senator Neville Bonner," Australian Broadcasting Corporation, 29 April 2012, https://www.abc.net.au/radionational/programs/archived/hindsight/compromise-and-confrontation/3972120.

[51] "Threats Against Neville Bonner and Aboriginal Establishments in Queensland," National Archives of Australia, circa 1971.

[52] "Bonner", Interviewed by Robyn Buchanan.

[53] Ibid.

[54] Senator Neville Bonner, *Commonwealth Parliamentary Debates*, Senate, 28 June 1974, p. 2984.

[55] Ibid.

[56] Bonner, "First Aboriginal in the Australian federal parliament: Interview with Robin Hughes."

[57] Senator John Woodley, *Commonwealth Parliamentary Debates*, Senate, 15 February 1999, p. 1842.

[58] Heather Bonner in Maureen Millar, "Warm-hearted Mr. Bonner Makes History" *Australian Women's Weekly*, 9 June 1971, p. 7.

[59] Bonner, "First Aboriginal in the Australian federal parliament: Interview with Robin Hughes."

[60] Rita Huggins and Jackie Huggins, "Activism," Auntie Rita, https://auntierita.weebly.com/activism.html.

[61] Ibid.

[62] Rita Huggins, *Auntie Rita*, Aboriginal Studies Press, 2005, p. 85.

[63] National Museum of Australia, https://www.nma.gov.au/explore/features/indigenous-rights/organisations/expansion-folder/fcaatsi.

[64] Burger, *Bonner*, p. 64.

[65] Bonner, Interviewed by Robyn Buchanan.

[66] Ibid.

67 Theodore R. Johnson, "Why are African-Americans such loyal Democrats when they are so ideologically diverse?" *The Washington Post*, 26 September 2016, https://www.washingtonpost.com/news/monkey-cage/wp/2016/09/28/can-trump-win-black-votes-what-we-know-from-5-decades-of-black-voting-data/.

68 Robert Menzies, *Afternoon Light: Some Memories of Men and Events*, Penguin Books, Ringwood, 1970, p. 292.

69 Ibid.

70 Burger, *Bonner*, p. 111.

71 Rowse, "Bonner, Neville Thomas (1922–1999)"; Senator Neville Bonner, *Commonwealth Parliamentary Debates*, Senate, 7 June 1973, p. 2479.

72 Senator Neville Bonner, *Commonwealth Parliamentary Debates*, Senate, 10 September 1975, p. 676.

73 Burger, *Bonner*, p. 63.

74 Trevor Ballantyne, "Sly racism in Queensland Senator Neville Bonner and the Country Party," *Politics*, Vol 8, No 1, 1973, pp. 155-157.

75 Burger, *Bonner*, p. 61.

76 Bonner, "First Aboriginal in the Australian federal parliament: Interview with Robin Hughes."

77 Ibid.

78 Burger, *Bonner*, p. 69.

79 "Senator the Honourable Dame Annabelle Rankin's resignation from the Senate - N T Bonner [Neville Bonner] to fill vacancy," National Archives of Australia, 9 November 1999, https://recordsearch.naa.gov.au/SearchNRetrieve/Interface/DetailsReports/ItemDetail.aspx?Barcode=4034108&isAv=N.

80 Ibid.

81 Ziems, "*Neville Bonner: Voice of a Broken People.*"

82 Senator Ian Macdonald, *Commonwealth Parliamentary Debates*, Senate, 15 February 1999, p. 1847.

83 Hugh Lunn, *Joh: The Life and Political Adventures of Johannes Bjelke-Pe-*

tersen, University of Queensland Press, St Lucia, 1978, p. xvi.

84 Bolton, *Spoils and Spoilers*, p. 163.

85 Joh Bjelke-Petersen, *Don't you worry about that!*, Angus and Robertson, North Ryde, 1990, p. 184.

86 Bonner, "First Aboriginal in the Australian federal parliament: Interview with Robin Hughes."

87 Ibid.

88 Lunn, *Joh*, p. 148.

89 Senator Neville Bonner, *Commonwealth Parliamentary Debates*, Senate, 5 February 1974, 3191. The following quotes are from the same session.

90 Senator Jim Keeffe, *Commonwealth Parliamentary Debates*, Senate, 5 February 1974, p. 3191.

91 Senator Neville Bonner, *Commonwealth Parliamentary Debates*, Senate, 5 February 1974, p. 3191.

92 Senator Neville Bonner, *Commonwealth Parliamentary Debates*, Senate, 27 May 1975, p. 1873.

93 Neville Bonner, Constitutional Convention 1998 – Day 3 – Hansard, Wednesday 4 February 1998, https://australianpolitics.com/issues/republic/convention/040298.pdf, p. 263.

94 Ibid., p. 262.

95 Ibid., p. 263.

96 Burger, *Bonner*, p. 131.

97 Ibid.

98 Ibid., p. 133.

99 Senator Neville Bonner, *Commonwealth Parliamentary Debates*, Senate, 8 December 1976, p. 2791.

100 Ibid.

101 Senator Neville Bonner, *Commonwealth Parliamentary Debates*, Senate, 15 March 1978, p. 596.

102 Bonner, "First Aboriginal in the Australian federal parliament: Interview with Robin Hughes."

103 Ibid.

104 Ibid.

105 Burger, *Bonner*, p. 153.

106 Jens Korff, "Aboriginal politicians" *Creative Spirits*, 27 November 2019, https://www.creativespirits.info/aboriginalculture/politics/aboriginal-politicians.

107 Personal correspondence, 2018.

108 Ibid.

109 John Howard (Prime Minister), *Neville Bonner Tribute Dinner*, Old Parliament House, Canberra, 31 May 2000, https://pmtranscripts.pmc.gov.au/release/transcript-22718.

110 Senator Ian Macdonald, *Commonwealth Parliamentary Debates*, Senate, 15 February 1999, p. 1847.

111 "Dumped Senator to stand as Independents" *Canberra Times*, 12 February 1983.

112 Kathryn Sullivan MP, *Commonwealth Parliamentary Debates*, House of Representatives, 27 September, 2001, p. 31666.

113 Ibid.

114 Ibid.

115 Bonner, Interviewed by Robyn Buchanan.

116 Chris Griffith, "Interview with Neville Bonner," Land Rights Queensland, April 1995, https://www.chrisgriffith.com/1990s/1995/nbonner.html.

117 Ibid.

118 Alexander Reilly, "Dedicated Seats in the Federal Parliament for Indigenous Australians: The Theoretical Case and its Practical Possibility," *Balayi: Culture, Law and* Colonialism, Vol 2, No 1, 2001, pp. 73-103.

119 Bonner, Interviewed by Robyn Buchanan.

120 Senator Ron Boswell, *Commonwealth Parliamentary Debates*, Senate, 15 February 1999, p. 1841.

121 Senator Ian Macdonald, *Commonwealth Parliamentary Debates*, Senate, 15 February 1999, p. 1847.

122 Ibid., p. 1837.

[123] Senator John Faulkner, *Commonwealth Parliamentary Debates*, Senate, 15 February 1999, p. 1837.

[124] Senator Ian Macdonald, *Commonwealth Parliamentary Debates*, Senate, 15 February 1999, p. 1847.

[125] Senator Warwick Parer *Commonwealth Parliamentary Debates*, Senate, 15 February 1999, p. 1845.

[126] Kwasi Kwarteng, "The role of the individual in the British Empire," *British Empire*, 22 May 2014, https://www.british-empire.co.uk/article/kwasikwartengaddress.htm.

[127] Neville Bonner, "Neville Thomas Bonner - Doctor of the University Occasional Speech," Griffith University, 1993, https://www.youtube.com/watch?v=fPqgAVFlj58.

[128] Edith Hall, *Aristotle's Way: How Ancient Wisdom Can Change Your Life*, The Bodley Head, London, 2018, p. 111.

[129] "Bonner", Interviewed by Robyn Buchanan.

[130] Senator Neville Bonner, *Commonwealth Parliamentary Debates*, Senate, 21 November 1973, p. 2016.

[131] Ibid., 2016. Here Bonner cites a letter from a constituent Mr Les Davidson of 825 Boonah Road, Churchill, Ipswich, Queensland: "I believe that a much more effective measure would be to make Aborigines more politically aware by means of education and publicity so that they enrol in State and Federal elections."

[132] Menzies, *Afternoon Light*, p. 296.

[133] Neville Bonner, "Interviewed by Pat Shaw Hughes for Oral History Project," National Library of Australia, 1983, https://nla.gov.au/nla.obj-217919415/listen.

www.ingramcontent.com/pod-product-compliance
Lightning Source LLC
Chambersburg PA
CBHW071626170426
43195CB00038B/2143